I have hidden your word in my heart that I might not sin against you.
Psalm 119:11.

100 creative

WAYS 2 LEARN

memory verses

KAREN HOLFORD

Autumn House® Publishing
www.autumnhousepublishing.com
A Division of **REVIEW AND HERALD® PUBLISHING**
Since 1861

Copyright © 2010 by General Conference of Seventh-day Adventists, Department of Children's Ministry

Published by Autumn House® Publishing, a division of Review and Herald® Publishing, Hagerstown, MD 21741-1119

Autumn House® titles may be purchased in bulk for educational, business, fund-raising, or sales promotional use. For information, please e-mail SpecialMarkets@reviewandherald.com.

Autumn House® Publishing publishes biblically based materials for spiritual, physical, and mental growth and Christian discipleship.

The author assumes full responsibility for the accuracy of all facts and quotations as cited in this book.

Unless otherwise noted, all Scripture references are from the *Holy Bible, New International Version*. Copyright © 1973, 1978, 1984, International Bible Society. Used by permission of Zondervan Bible Publishers.

This book was
Edited by Kalie Kelch
Cover designed by Ron J. Pride
Interior designed by Tina Ivany
Cover illustration by Ron J. Pride
Typeset: Bembo 11/14

PRINTED IN U.S.A.

14 13 12 11 10   5 4 3 2 1

Library of Congress Cataloging-in-Publication Data

Holford, Karen.
  100 creative ways to learn memory verses / Karen Holford.
    p. cm.
  Includes bibliographical references and index.
  1. Bible—Memorizing. 2. Bible—Study and teaching. 3. Christian education of children. I. Title. II. Title: One hundred creative ways to learn memory verses.
  BS617.7.H65 2010
  268'.432—dc22
                        2009047633

ISBN 978-0-8127-0505-8
Library of Congress Cataloging-in-Publication Data

ISBN 978-0-8127-0505-8

To order additional copies of *100 Creative Ways to Learn Memory Verses,* by Karen Holford, call **1-800-765-6955.**

Visit us at **www.AutumnHousePublishing.com** for information on other Autumn House® products.

with many thanks to

Beth Holford, my daughter,
for fine-tuning the almost finished manuscript.

Bernie Holford, my husband,
who helped me to find elusive Bible verses
and provided the information on the different Bible versions.

Nathan and Joel Holford, my sons,
who fed us amazing variations on the theme of pasta
while this book was in progress.

contents

Foreword

K aren Holford, my friend and colleague in ministry, is passionate about children. She has served as associate director of children's ministries for the Seventh-day Adventist Church in the South England Conference for many years. Her great dream is that our churches will seriously think that children matter and actively involve them in all aspects of the church life.

In *100 Creative Ways to Learn Memory Verses* Karen offers many interesting ways of grounding our children in Scripture learning. She believes this is crucial because there is an invisible battle going on—a spiritual war that rages over each and every child. The reason for this raging warfare is very clear. Recent research by the George Barna Group indicates that the vast majority of people who become Christians do so while still children, usually before the age of 14. If a person hasn't accepted Jesus as a teenager, the probability he or she will ever know Jesus is only 23 percent.

This is just one of the many books and articles Karen has written to help parents and teachers in nurturing our children in their journey with Jesus Christ. Using the ideas in this book will change your method of teaching and stimulate children in knowing the Word of God. You and your children will be blessed!

—Linda Mei Lin Koh, Director
Children's Ministries
General Conference of Seventh-day Adventists

Before you start . . .

The Word of God is at the very center of our relationship with Him, and learning memory verses embeds His scriptures in our hearts. The Bible verses in this book will speak of His love, wisdom, peace, encouragement, comfort, and guidance throughout our lives. The Bible passages and verses that we memorize add to the voice of the Holy Spirit, and enabling Him to more easily bring these verses to our minds when He knows we need them.

Helping our children to learn key verses and passages of Scripture is a vital part of their spiritual nurture, growth, and discipling process. A hundred years ago children would have been accustomed to learning information by rote—repeating words over and over until they were word perfect. It worked well for children who could memorize quickly or who were good at remembering what they heard or saw, but today's children are often taught in multisensory ways, and many of us learn best by *doing* something, rather than by hearing or seeing words.

It is also very important to help children understand the meaning of the verses. As a child I was required to learn Psalm 23, a classic piece that I can still remember quite well (on a good day). The words, however, were bewildering for me, especially in the King James Version. "The Lord is my Shepherd I shall not want" is what I heard, and I wondered why there was a verse in the Bible that said I shouldn't want God. Rote learning can help children to learn the words but not necessarily the meaning, and we need to give them the opportunity to discuss the verses and how they apply to their lives today.

In my job as an occupational therapist, I spent several years working with people who had difficulties with their memory. We discovered that our clients remembered things better when they experienced something for themselves, when they were involved in the process, when they were enjoying themselves, or when there was a higher-than-usual level of adrenalin in their body. They were also able to remember things better if the learning was repeated in new and interesting ways, and if they could see, hear, and do something with the information they were trying to remember. Our clients were more likely to remember things that they understood and information that they had discussed with other people.

In this book I have used the information about memory that I've gathered as an occupational therapist and have included many different activities to encourage the memorization of Bible verses. Hopefully you will find ideas in this book to suit a variety of interests, skills, learning styles, group sizes, and available materials. I have also included a selection of key verses to get you started, but many of the activities are suitable for any Bible verse that your child may need to learn.

Here are a few tips to bear in mind when using a memory verse activity from this book:

- Choose verses that are relevant to the ages and needs of the children in your family or group.
- Interpret them to suit your own situation and requirements. Some activities in the book have been worded as if they are for larger groups of children in a class, and others for smaller groups, such as a family. Interpret them to suit your own situation and requirements.
- Explore the verse for yourself. What does it mean to you? When has this verse been useful for you? Why is this verse important to learn? Reflect on the verse and pray for understanding before sharing it with the children.
- Choose an activity from the book that has a link to the verse, if possible, so that the *way* the verse is learned is connected with the *meaning* of the verse being learned.
- Make sure you understand the instructions, and check that the activity works smoothly in your context, before trying to teach the children. Complications, interruptions, or things that don't work well are very distracting to the memorization process and disheartening for both you and the children.
- Make a sample of any finished products so that the children can see what they are aiming to achieve.
- Where appropriate, have clear copies of the verse available for the children so they can refer to them during the activity.
- Emphasize enjoyment and creativity when using the memorization activities rather than competition and perfection.
- Use the ideas in this book to spark your own variations and you will soon have many more than 100 ideas at you fingertips!

Ideas for Bible Verses to Learn

1. Ten Verses About God
2. Ten Verses About Jesus
3. Ten Verses About the Holy Spirit
4. Ten Verses About Salvation
5. Ten Verses About Faith
6. Ten Verses About Love
7. Ten Verses of Wisdom
8. Ten Verses About Relationships
9. Ten Verses of Promise
10. Ten Verses About Children
11. Ten Foundations of Faith
12. Ten Classic Passages

Following are a selection of Bible verses that may be useful for children (or adults) to learn. These are just a few of the many wonderful verses that could be chosen. The Bible is packed full of wisdom, teaching, and encouragement. Use these verses as a starting point, and develop your own list of relevant verses.

The verses and passages on the following pages are all taken from the New International Version of the Bible, which is used in many churches. If you have access to a special children's translation, this could provide you with an alternate version of the verses that children may be able to understand better. However, as children mature they will develop a richer understanding of the verses they learned when they were young, and it may be helpful for them to memorize the verses in a version that is familiar to others in their spiritual culture.

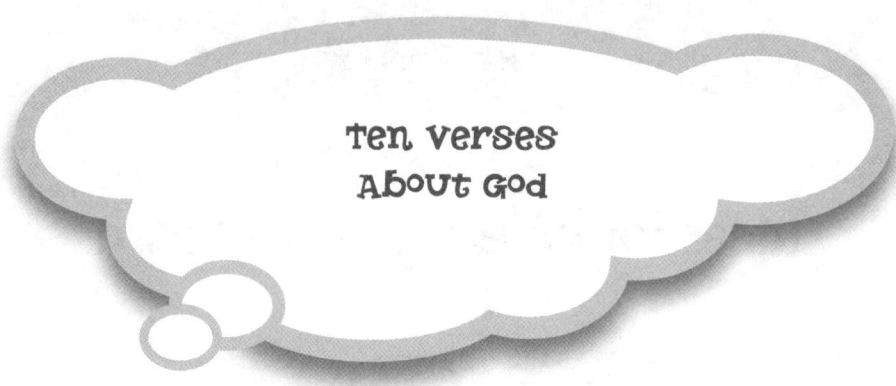

Ten Verses About God

1. "God is our refuge and strength, an ever-present help in trouble" (Ps. 46:1).

2. "So do not fear, for I am with you; do not be dismayed, for I am your God. I will strengthen you and help you; I will uphold you with my righteous right hand" (Isa. 41:10).

3. "I, even I, am he who blots out your transgressions, for my own sake, and remembers your sins no more" (Isa. 43:25).

4. "I am God, and there is no other; I am God, and there is none like me" (Isa. 46:9).

5. "'Though the mountains be shaken and the hills be removed, yet my unfailing love for you will not be shaken nor my covenant of peace be removed,' says the Lord, who has compassion on you" (Isa. 54:10).

6. "Surely your God is the God of gods and the Lord of kings and a revealer of mysteries, for you were able to reveal this mystery" (Dan. 2:47).

7. "And we know that in all things God works for the good of those who love him, who have been called according to his purpose" (Rom. 8:28).

8. "For I am convinced that neither death nor life, neither angels nor demons, neither the present nor the future, nor any powers, neither height nor depth, nor anything else in all creation, will be able to separate us from the love of God that is in Christ Jesus our Lord" (Rom. 8:38, 39).

9. "God is faithful; he will not let you be tempted beyond what you can bear. But when you are tempted, he will also provide a way out so that you can stand up under it" (1 Cor. 10:13).

10. "Praise be to the God and Father of our Lord Jesus Christ, the Father of compassion and the God of all comfort, who comforts us in all our troubles, so that we can comfort those in any trouble with the comfort we ourselves have received from God" (2 Cor. 1:3, 4).

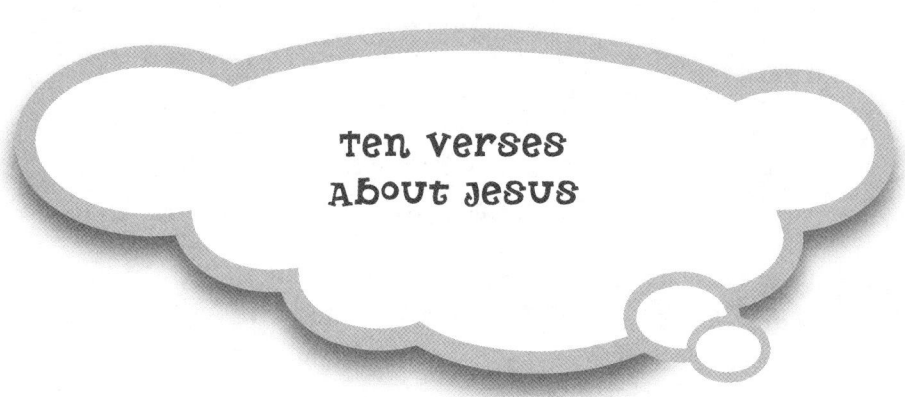

Ten Verses About Jesus

1. "For to us a child is born, to us a son is given, and the government will be on his shoulders. And he will be called Wonderful Counselor, Mighty God, Everlasting Father, Prince of Peace" (Isa. 9:6).
2. "But he was pierced for our transgressions, he was crushed for our iniquities; the punishment that brought us peace was upon him, and by his wounds we are healed" (Isa. 53:5).
3. "And Jesus grew in wisdom and stature, and in favor with God and men" (Luke 2:52).
4. "The Word became flesh and made his dwelling among us" (John 1:14).
5. "I am the good shepherd; I know my sheep and my sheep know me—just as the Father knows me and I know the Father—and I lay down my life for the sheep" (John 10:14, 15).
6. "But I, when I am lifted up from the earth, will draw all men to myself" (John 12:32).
7. "Jesus answered, 'I am the way and the truth and the life. No one comes to the Father except through me'" (John 14:6).
8. "For we do not have a high priest who is unable to sympathize with our weaknesses, but we have one who has been tempted in every way, just as we are—yet was without sin" (Heb. 4:15).
9. "And this is the testimony: God has given us eternal life, and this life is in his Son. He who has the Son has life; he who does not have the Son of God does not have life" (1 John 5:11, 12).
10. "Here I am! I stand at the door and knock. If anyone hears my voice and opens the door, I will come in and eat with him, and he with me" (Rev. 3:20).

Ten Verses About the Holy Spirit

1. "I will pour out my Spirit on all people. Your sons and daughters will prophesy, your old men will dream dreams, your young men will see visions" (Joel 2:28).

2. "At that moment heaven was opened, and he saw the Spirit of God descending like a dove and lighting on him, And a voice from heaven said, 'This is my Son, whom I love; with him I am well pleased'" (Matt. 3:16, 17).

3. "I tell you the truth, no one can enter the kingdom of God unless he is born of water and the Spirit" (John 3:5).

4. "The wind blows wherever it pleases. You hear its sound, but you cannot tell where it comes from or where it is going. So it is with everyone born of the Spirit" (John 3:8).

5. "But the Counselor, the Holy Spirit, whom the Father will send in my name, will teach you all things and will remind you of everything I have said to you" (John 14:26).

6. "Peter replied, 'Repent and be baptized, every one of you, in the name of Jesus Christ for the forgiveness of your sins. And you will receive the gift of the Holy Spirit'" (Acts 2:38).

7. "Do you not know that you body is a temple of the Holy Spirit, who is in you, whom you have received from God? You are not your own; you were bought at a price. Therefore honor God with your body" (1 Cor. 6:19, 20).

8. "There are different kinds of gifts, but the same Spirit. There are different kinds of service, but the same Lord. . . . All these are the work of one and the same Spirit, and he gives them to each one, just as he determines" (1 Cor. 12:4–11).

9. "But the fruit of the Spirit is love, joy, peace, patience, kindness, goodness, faithfulness, gentleness and self-control. Against such things there is no law" (Gal. 5:22, 23).

10. "For prophecy never had its origin in the will of man, but men spoke from God as they were carried along by the Holy Spirit" (2 Peter 1:21).

ten verses About salvation

1. "For God so loved the world that he gave his one and only Son, that whoever believes in him shall not perish but have eternal life" (John 3:16).
2. "Jesus answered, 'I am the way and the truth and the life. No one comes to the Father except through me'" (John 14:6).
3. "Remain in me, and I will remain in you. No branch can bear fruit by itself; it must remain in the vine. Neither can you bear fruit unless you remain in m" (John 15:4).
4. "Now this is eternal life: that they may know you, the only true God, and Jesus Christ, whom you have sent" (John 17:3).
5. "For all have sinned and fall short of the glory of God" (Rom. 3:23).
6. "But God demonstrates his own love for us in this: While we were still sinners, Christ died for us" (Rom. 5:8).
7. "For the wages of sin is death, but the gift of God is eternal life in Christ Jesus our Lord" (Rom. 6:23).
8. "For it is by grace you have been saved, through faith—and this not from yourselves, it is the gift of God—not by works, so that no one can boast" (Eph. 2:8, 9).
9. "Therefore, if anyone is in Christ, he is a new creation; the old has gone, the new has come!" (2 Cor. 5:17).
10. "And God is able to make all grace abound to you, so that in all things at all times, having all that you need, you will abound in every good work" (2 Cor. 9:8).

Ten Verses About Faith

1. "Jesus looked at them and said, 'With man this is impossible, but not with God; all things are possible with God'" (Mark 10:27).

2. "Therefore I tell you, whatever you ask for in prayer, believe that you have received it, and it will be yours" (Mark 11:24).

3. "If you have faith as small as a mustard seed, you can say to this mulberry tree, 'Be uprooted and planted in the sea,' and it will obey you" (Luke 17:6).

4. "I tell you the truth, anyone who has faith in me will do what I have been doing. He will do even greater things than these, because I am going to the Father" (John 14:12).

5. "Then Jesus told him [Thomas], 'Because you have seen me, you have believed; blessed are those who have not seen and yet have believed'" (John 20:29).

6. "So we fix our eyes not on what is seen, but on what is unseen. For what is seen is temporary, but what is unseen is eternal" (2 Cor. 4:18).

7. "We live by faith, not by sight" (2 Cor. 5:7).

8. "Now faith is being sure of what we hope for and certain of what we do not see" (Heb. 11:1).

9. "Though you have not seen him, you love him; and even though you do not see him now, you believe in him and are filled with an inexpressible and glorious joy, for you are receiving the goal of your faith, the salvation of your souls" (1 Peter 1:8, 9).

10. "This is the confidence we have in approaching God: that if we ask anything according to his will, he hears us. And if we know that he hears us—whatever we ask—we know that we have what we asked of him" (1 John 5:14, 15).

Ten Verses About Love

1. "A friend loves at all times" (Prov. 17:17).
2. "Many waters cannot quench love; rivers cannot wash it away" (S. of Sol. 8:7).
3. "Love your enemies and pray for those who persecute you, that you may be the sons of your Father in heaven" (Matt. 5:44, 45).
4. "A new command I give you: Love one another. As I have loved you, so you must love one another. By this all men will know that you are my disciples, if you love one another" (John 13:34, 35).
5. "Greater love has no one than this, that he lay down his life for his friends" (John15:13).
6. "The entire law is summed up in a single command: 'Love your neighbor as yourself'" (Gal. 5:14).
7. "How great is the love the Father has lavished on us, that we should be called children of God! And that is what we are!" (1 John 3:1).
8. "Dear children, let us not love with words or tongue but with actions and in truth" (1 John 3:18).
9. "Whoever does not love does not know God, because God is love" (1 John 4:8).
10. "There is no fear in love. But perfect love drives out fear, because fear has to do with punishment" (1 John 4:18).

Ten Verses of Wisdom

1. "He has showed you, O man, what is good. And what does the Lord require of you? To act justly and to love mercy and to walk humbly with your God" (Micah 6:8).

2. "For the foolishness of God is wiser than man's wisdom, and the weakness of God is stronger than man's strength" (1 Cor. 1:25).

3. "Do you not know that your body is a temple of the Holy Spirit, who is in you, whom you have received from God? You are not your own; you were bought at a price. Therefore honor God with your body" (1 Cor. 6:19, 20).

4. "Remember this: Whoever sows sparingly will also reap sparingly, and whoever sows generously will also reap generously" (2 Cor. 9:6).

5. "Finally, brothers, whatever is true, whatever is noble, whatever is right, whatever is pure, whatever is lovely, whatever is admirable—if anything is excellent or praiseworthy—think about such things" (Phil. 4:8).

6. "Whatever you do, work at it with all your heart, as working for the Lord, not for men, since you know that you will receive an inheritance from the Lord as a reward. It is the Lord Christ you are serving" (Col. 3:23, 24).

7. "Make it your ambition to lead a quiet life, to mind your own business and to work with your hands, just as we told you, so that your daily life may win the respect of outsiders and so that you will not be dependent on anybody" (1 Thess. 4:11, 12).

8. "For the love of money is a root of all kinds of evil" (1 Tim. 6:10).

9. "Don't have anything to do with foolish and stupid arguments, because you know they produce quarrels" (2 Tim. 2:23).

10. "But the wisdom that comes from heaven is first of all pure; then peace-loving, considerate, submissive, full of mercy and good fruit, impartial and sincere" (James 3:17).

Ten Verses About Relationships

1. "Rejoice with those who rejoice; mourn with those who mourn. Live in harmony with one another. Do not be proud, but be willing to associate with people of low position. Do not be conceited" (Rom. 12:15, 16).

2. "If it is possible, as far as it depends on you, live at peace with everyone" (Rom. 12:18).

3. "Do not let any unwholesome talk come out of your mouths, but only what is helpful for building others up according to their needs, that it may benefit those who listen" (Eph. 4:29).

4. "Be kind and compassionate to one another, forgiving each other, just as in Christ God forgave you" (Eph. 4:32).

5. "Do nothing out of selfish ambition or vain conceit, but in humility consider others better than yourselves. Each of you should look not only to your own interests, but also to the interests of others" (Phil. 2:3, 4).

6. "Do everything without complaining or arguing, so that you may become blameless and pure, children of God without fault in a crooked and depraved generation, in which you shine like stars in the universe" (Phil. 2:14, 15).

7. "Bear with each other and forgive whatever grievances you may have against one another. Forgive as the Lord forgave you. And over all these virtues put on love, which binds them all together in perfect unity" (Col. 3:13, 14).

8. "Therefore encourage one another and build each other up, just as in fact you are doing" (1 Thess. 5:11).

9. "Do not forget to entertain strangers, for by so doing some people have entertained angels without knowing it" (Heb. 13:2).

10. "My dear brothers, take note of this: Everyone should be quick to listen, slow to speak and slow to become angry" (James 1:19).

Ten verses of promise

1. "The angel of the LORD encamps around those who fear him, and he delivers them" (Ps. 34:7).
2. "You will keep in perfect peace him whose mind is steadfast, because he trusts in you" (Isa. 26:3).
3. "Those who hope in the LORD will renew their strength. They will soar on wings like eagles; they will run and not grow weary, they will walk and not be faint" (Isa. 40:31).
4. "'For I know the plans I have for you,' declares the Lord, 'plans to prosper you and not to harm you, plans to give you hope and a future'" (Jer. 29:11).
5. "Therefore do not worry about tomorrow, for tomorrow will worry about itself. Each day has enough trouble of its own" (Matt. 6:34).
6. "Ask and it will be given to you; seek and you will find; knock and the door will be opened to you. For everyone who asks receives; he who seeks finds; and to him who knocks, the door will be opened" (Matt. 7:7, 8).
7. "It is written: 'No eye has seen, no ear has heard, no mind has conceived what God has prepared for those who love him'" (1 Cor. 2:9).
8. "I can do everything through him who gives me strength" (Phil. 4:13).
9. "Consider it pure joy, my brothers, whenever you face trials of many kinds, because you know that the testing of your faith develops perseverance" (James 1:2, 3).
10. "He will wipe every tear from their eyes. There will be no more death or mourning or crying or pain, for the old order of things has passed away" (Rev. 21:4).

ten verses About children

1. "Then Samuel said, 'Speak, for your servant is listening'" (1 Sam. 3:10).
2. "For you created my inmost being; you knit me together in my mother's womb. I praise you because I am fearfully and wonderfully made; your works are wonderful" (Ps. 139:13, 14).
3. "Even a child is known by his actions, by whether his conduct is pure and right" (Prov. 20:11).
4. "Train a child in the way he should go, and when he is old he will not turn from it"(Prov. 22:6).
5. "Remember your Creator in the days of your youth" (Eccl. 12:1).
6. "And he said: 'I tell you the truth, unless you change and become like little children, you will never enter the kingdom of heaven'" (Matt. 18:3).
7. "See that you do not look down on any of these little ones. For I tell you that their angels in heaven always see the face of my Father in heaven" (Matt. 18:10).
8. "Let the little children come to me, and do not hinder them, for the kingdom of God belongs to such as these" (Luke 18:16).
9. "Children, obey your parents in the Lord, for this is right. 'Honor your father and mother'—which is the first commandment with a promise—'that it may go well with you and that you may enjoy long life on the earth'" (Eph. 6:1-3).
10. "Don't let anyone look down on you because you are young, but set an example for the believers in speech, in life, in love, in faith and in purity" (1 Tim. 4:12).

Ten Foundations
of Faith

1. "In the beginning God created the heavens and the earth" (Gen. 1:1).

2. "For the living know that they will die, but the dead know nothing" (Eccl. 9:5).

3. "If you call the Sabbath a delight and the LORD's holy day honorable, and if you honor it by not going your own way and not doing as you please or speaking idle words, then you will find your joy in the LORD" (Isa. 58:13, 14).

4. "No one knows about that day or hour, not even the angels in heaven, nor the Son, but only the Father. . . . Therefore keep watch, because you do not know on what day your Lord will come" (Matt. 24:36, 42).

5. "Therefore go and make disciples of all nations, baptizing them in the name of the Father and of the Son and of the Holy Spirit, and teaching them to obey everything I have commanded you" (Matt. 28:19, 20).

6. "At that time men will see the Son of Man coming in clouds with great power and glory. And he will send his angels and gather his elect from the four winds, from the ends of the earth to the ends of the heavens" (Mark 13:26, 27).

7. "For everything that was written in the past was written to teach us, so that through endurance and the encouragement of the Scriptures we might have hope" (Rom. 15:4).

8. "For Christ's love compels us, because we are convinced that one died for all, and therefore all died. And he died for all, that those who live should no longer live for themselves but for him who died for them and was raised again" (2 Cor. 5:14, 15).

9. "For the Lord himself will come down from heaven, with a loud command, with the voice of the archangel and with the trumpet call of God, and the dead in Christ will rise first. After that, we who are still alive and are left will be caught up with them in the clouds to meet the Lord in the air. And so we will be with the Lord forever" (1 Thess. 4:16, 17).

10. "This calls for patient endurance on the part of the saints who obey God's commandments and remain faithful to Jesus" (Rev. 14:12).

Ten Classic Passages

1. The Ten Commandments: Exodus 20:1-17.
2. The Blessings of God's Law: Psalm 19:7-11.
3. The Shepherd's Psalm: Psalm 23.
4. The Character of God: Psalm 103.
5. New Heavens and a New Earth: Isaiah 65:17-25.
6. The Beatitudes: Matthew 5:3-12.
7. The Lord's Prayer: Matthew 6:9-13.
8. The Love Chapter: 1 Corinthians 13.
9. The Humility of Christ: Philippians 2:6-11.
10. God's Love and Ours: 1 John 4:7-18.

Ten Ways to Learn Memory Verses Using Games

1. Bible Verse Memory Game/Matching Game
2. Pass the Parcel
3. Verse Towers
4. Alphabetti Verse
5. Verse on a Line
6. String Trail
7. Fishing for Words
8. Jacob's Ladder
9. Hide a Verse
10. Memory Verse Bingo

1. Bible Verse Memory Game/Matching Game

Use with verses about gifts or blessings.

Supplies:

- one sheet of paper with the full Bible verse written on it
- one pack of plain index cards
- markers

Instructions:

1. Write each word of the verse on a seperate index card.
2. Write the complete Bible verse on an index card and position it so that everyone can see it.
3. Shuffle the individual cards and lay them face down on the table or floor so all the words are hidden. Take turns picking up a card and reading the word that is written on it. If the word that is picked is not the next word needed in the verse, return it to its place, face down. Then let the next player have a turn.
4. Lay down the first word of the verse when it has been picked up, and start building the verse.
5. When someone picks up a correct word, the card is placed beside the previous card, and the player takes another turn at finding the next card.
6. Continue the game until all the words have been found and laid out in order.

Other ideas:

- Write several words on each card for longer verses or passages of Scripture instead of one word on each card, depending on how long you want the activity to last.
- Write several verses on cards so that you have one verse per player. Write two words on some cards to adjust the length of the verses. Shuffle the cards and lay them out on the floor as before. Give each person a different verse to complete. If one player picks up the next word in another player's sequence, he gives the card to the other player and takes another turn, unless it is the next word he needs for his own verse.

2. pass the parcel

Use with verses about growing,
building each other up, sharing, and helping.

supplies:

- newspapers or sheets of newsprint
- tape
- a pack of plain index cards
- a package to be wrapped in the middle of the parcel, with enough treats for each player
- a tape or CD
- a tape or CD player

instructions:

1. Write each word of the verse on a different index card. (It is best if there are 12 cards or less. Write two words on some of the cards, if necessary.)
2. Stack the cards in the correct order with the Bible text on the top and the first word at the bottom of the pile.
3. Place the treats inside the package and wrap it in newsprint. Stick the Bible text firmly to the package of treats, then wrap this package in another layer of paper and stick the next card in your pile firmly to the new wrapping.
4. Continue attaching one of the word cards to each layer of wrapping. Add a final layer of wrapping so all the words are hidden.
5. Play "Pass the Parcel" with the package you have created by seating the players in a circle and playing music as the package is passed from one person to the next.
6. Stop the music after a short time. Whoever is holding the package when the music stops is invited to remove one layer of wrapping and read the word(s) written on the index card.

7. Start the music again and let the children pass the package around the circle. Each child has to say the word that was just read before they pass the package to the next child. The music continues to stop and start, and the players continue to take off the layers of paper to reveal new words. As more words are revealed, the players have to quote the memory verse up to that point before they can pass the package to the next person.

8. Have the players say the whole verse together when they reach the last card, which is the Bible text.

9. Unwrap the final layer to reveal the treats. Share the treats with everyone!

Other ideas:

- Include some objects or pictures that illustrate some of the words in the text, such as a small birthday candle for "light," a heart shaped eraser for "heart," or a picture of the world for "world."
- Choose treats that connect with the theme of the verse to give children an extra reminder of the verse and its meaning.
- Design bookmarks on your computer using the verse that is being learned and laminate them to give as treats.

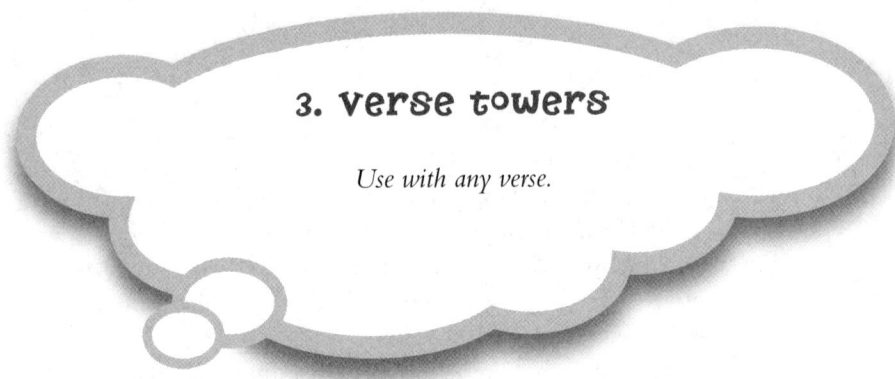

3. verse towers

Use with any verse.

supplies:

- a selection of similar sized boxes, such as shoe boxes
- wrapping paper, newsprint, or brown paper for wrapping the boxes
- index cards and markers or a computer, printer, and paper for printing out the words and reference of the memory verse
- a copy of the memory verse for each team of players

instructions:

1. Wrap each box firmly in paper.
2. Attach one word of the memory verse to one of the long sides of each box.
3. Make a set of boxes for each team, and give each team the boxes in a disorganized heap.
4. Give them a copy of the complete verse to guide them, if you wish, or see how close they can get to the verse by rearranging the boxes without the verse to guide them.
5. See how quickly they can make a tower of their verse with the first word at the top of the tower and the text at the bottom.

other ideas:

- Give an extra box to each group that contains some small gifts with Bible verses on them, such as balloons, stickers, erasers, etc. Or hide the gifts in one of the word boxes.
- Turn some of the boxes around so some of the words are hidden, and see if the children can remember the hidden words. Play this missing word game after the tower has been made and the children have read the verse. Continue to turn the boxes around until all the words are hidden and the children can say the verse without any prompts.

- Use several different verses, and give each group a set of boxes, half of which are their own and half that belong to another group. The players then have to swap words with the other teams until they get the ones they need. Then they can build their towers.
- Recycle the boxes to use with different verses. Cover them with clear adhesive film for increased durability, and attach the words with removable adhesive putty.

4. Alphabetti verse

Use with verses about God's leading and guidance.

supplies:

- a bag of alphabet pasta from a specialist food shop or Italian delicatessen
- a printout of the Bible verse for each person
- a small bowl for each person

Instructions:

1. Give each person a small bowl of pasta letter shapes and a copy of the Bible verse.
2. Have each person search through his/her pasta shapes to find the letters he/she needs to build the verse until all the letters have been found and arranged to spell out the entire verse.

Please note: Not every language uses all the letters we use in English, so there may be some letters missing from the alphabet pasta, such as W and Y. Check out what letters may be missing and then offer the children other possibilities for these letters, or use a verse that doesn't contain these letters. This activity requires concentration, patience, and fine motor skills, so you may need to offer an alternative activity for children who need to be more active or who would find this activity particularly challenging.

other ideas:

- Let the children cover a piece of card stock with white craft glue and stick the letters on the paper to spell out the verse. These verses can then be sprayed gold and decorated with craft materials to create attractive pictures.
- Press the letters into air-drying clay and create a plaque to hang on the wall.

5. verse on a Line

*Use with verses about being forgiven (washed clean)
and how God clothes us better than
He clothes the flowers of the field.*

supplies:

- a clothesline in the garden or a string tied across the room
- a selection of colored poster boards
- markers
- scissors
- clothespins
- baskets

Instructions:

1. Hang a clothesline or rope across the room.
2. Cut poster boards into the shapes of different clothes, such as T-shirts, pants, skirts, etc. Make them as big as your poster board will allow.
3. Write a different word of the verse on each garment.
4. Shuffle the garments and place them in a small basket, as if they are a pile of clean laundry.
5. Give each person, or group, a basket of words, and a pile of clothespins.
6. See how quickly they can pin their words on the line in the correct order to make the Bible verse and text. Then have them stand back from the line and read the verse out loud.

Other ideas:

- Use small circular drying racks (often used for drying smaller items of clothing) if you have limited space, and have the children pin the words in order around the drying rack.

- Let the children make miniature versions of these lines using string, smaller clothes shapes, and paper clips. Their line can then be hung as a garland in their bedroom or in a place where they will see it often, thus reminding them of the verse. The children could also collect a variety of words on clothes shapes and keep them in a small basket so the children could change their verses whenever they wanted to.
- Pin the cardboard clothing words onto the front of each child, and see if they can arrange themselves in the right order to create the verse.

6. String Trail

Use with any verse.

Supplies:

- a ball of string for each person
- a pack of luggage labels or tie on price tags
- markers
- Popsicle sticks
- little treats (optional)

Instructions:

(This is best done in small groups and can be done outside in a park or yard.)

1. Write each word of the verse on one of the tags or labels.
2. Take one ball of string, and lay it out in a wiggly route around the area. As you go, tie the words in order along the length of the string.
3. Tie a small reward at the end of the string.
4. Make a different string trail for each child.
5. Weave the strings around each other in some places to add some extra fun and challenge.
6. Give each child the beginning of a string trail and a Popsicle stick so they can wind their string around their stick as they go. Make sure the children don't see this as a race so that they take their time and move carefully around each other and any objects. Watch them to make sure no one gets hurt by the string.
7. Have the children stop and read all the words they find, in order. Before they can open their final treat, they need to come to you and say their verse without looking at the labels.

other ideas:

- Make one trail and let the children take turns rolling up the string between the words. Encourage them to say the words of the verse together each time a new word is found. Include enough treats at the end of the trail for each child to have one.
- Hide objects that may be mentioned in the Bible verse along the route of the string. Put them in unusual places. This helps those who are visual learners to remember the verse and makes the trail more interesting and surprising for everyone.

7. Fishing for words

Use with verses about water and fish.

Supplies:

- colored poster board (perhaps gold or orange for goldfish or other colors for different fish shapes)
- some simple fish templates
- pencils, scissors, and markers
- paper clips
- dowel rods
- string
- U-shaped magnets
- a clean, dry bucket or baby bath

Instructions:

1. Cut a variety of fish shapes out of the colored poster board. Write a word of the verse on each one and attach a paper clip to its mouth area.
2. Make fishing rods using the dowels, string, and magnets. You may need to screw a metal "eye" into the end of the dowel rod so you can tie the string to it. Tie the magnet to the other end of the string.
3. Place the fish in a bucket and let the children take turns fishing.
4. Lay the caught fish in a line to make the verse.

Other ideas:

- Make a different colored set of fish for each child.
- Add some extra, unwanted fish with words that the children won't need and will have to throw back in the "water."
- Give each child a large sheet of blue poster board, glue, plastic wrap, glitter, paint, etc., with which to create a watery ocean background. Then let them stick their word fish on the ocean background in the correct order to create a poster of their verse.

8. Jacob's Ladder

*Use with verses about
growing closer to God, angels, etc.*

Supplies:

- a large sheet of paper (the back of a roll of wallpaper is useful)
- thick markers
- putty adhesive for attaching the wallpaper to the wall (or use a chalkboard, whiteboard, overhead projector, etc.)

Instructions:

1. Draw two long lines on the back of the wallpaper to create the two sides of a ladder. Make some small marks along the sides of the ladder to show where you will draw the rungs. Mark the lines for 20 rungs. Fix this piece of paper to the wall where everyone can see it.
2. Take another piece of wallpaper, lay it out horizontally, and draw one line to represent each letter of each word in the verse, with wider spaces between the words (a three letter word would be three lines with a space between that word and the next word).
3. Explain to the children that they need to try and guess the words in the memory verse.
4. Let the children guess what words are in the memory verse. If a child correctly guesses a word in the verse, write the word in its correct place wherever it appears in the verse (if a word occurs more than once, write all of them in the verse after the child guesses that word).
5. Draw one rung on the ladder for every wrong guess. Fill in a different rung each time a wrong word is suggested. The goal is for the children to guess all the words in the verse before you finish drawing the rungs on Jacob's ladder.

Other ideas:

- Write the first letter of each word or all the Es, etc., to give the children extra clues if they find it hard to guess or if you want a quicker game.
- Let the child who guessed the verse first complete the rungs. Then let each player stick the laminated picture of an angel on the ladder using putty adhesive. Save the angels to use next time you play.
- Make a more permanent ladder with repositionable "rungs" so that you can reuse the game without having to draw a new ladder each time.
- Adapt the image to suit the verse you are trying to teach, such as a tree, a fortress, or a suit of armor.
- Build your ladder using construction toys, or print a simple rungless ladder on a piece of paper using your computer. Laminate the page so that the rungs can be drawn with a nonpermanent marker and wiped clean for reuse.

9. Hide-a-verse

*Use with verses about searching
and discovery.*

Supplies:

- a supply of different colored index cards
- scissors
- markers
- putty adhesive

Instructions:

1. Choose a Bible verse and divide it into 10 sections. Write each section on a separate card, using a different color for each verse set you create. If possible, use a different color for each child or for each team of children, if you have a larger group.
2. Hide the cards all over the area in which you will play the game. Use the putty adhesive to help you hide some of the cards under chairs, etc.
3. Give each player, or group of players, a different colored blank card, and ask them to find another 10 cards of the same color and rearrange them to create a Bible verse.

Other ideas:

- Create a simple treasure hunt with clues to help guide the children from one card to the next. Write the verse section on one side of the card and the clue on the other side.
- Reuse the cards for different age levels or groups by laminating them or covering them with protective film to make them more durable.

10. Memory Verse Bingo

Use with any verse.

Supplies:

- a computer and printer or a ruler and a pencil
- photocopier
- scissors
- thin card stock
- a small cloth bag

Instructions:

1. Use the computer or a pencil and ruler to create a simple grid four squares across and five squares down, for a total of 20 squares. Each square/rectangle needs to be the same size.
2. Write the words of the text within the grid, approximately one word per square. If necessary, write two words on some squares so the verse fits exactly within the grid.
3. Make two copies of every verse that you use.
4. Make a different verse for each player. You can have up to six players.
5. Take one copy of each verse and cut it up along the gridlines to create 20 small cards per verse. Put all the small cards into the fabric bag and shake the bag well so the words are all mixed up.
6. Give each player one of the intact grid cards. Taking turns, each player draws a card from the bag. If the card matches a square on their grid, they can keep the card and place it on their grid card. If they pick a card that does not fit on their grid, they return the word to the bag.
7. Continue until every grid is filled. Then the players can swap grid cards and play again so they can learn another verse.

Other ideas:

- Use pictures instead of words for some of the verses. Draw a simple object or insert a computer image as you create the grid.
- Use a picture that suits the verse and resize it to fill the whole grid, and then add the words from the verse on top of the picture. Print a plain grid with just the words on it to use as the grid card, and cut up the pictorial grid. This way, a picture will slowly develop, like a jigsaw, as the game progresses.
- Keep this game to reuse as a family activity.
- Make a game kit with several grid cards and a bag of small word cards for the children to take home and play with their family and friends. This is a good idea for a children's program activity.

Ten Ways to Learn Memory Verses Using Writing and Words

11. Picture Writing

12. Jigsaw Verse

13. Disappearing Verse

14. Secret Codes

15. Newspaper Verse

16. Crossword/Wordsearch Puzzle

17. Join the Dots Verse

18. Calligraphic Verse

19. Minibook Verse

20. Verse Response

11. Picture Writing

*Use with verses that suggest
a pictorial image.*

Supplies:

- sheets of paper
- pencils and crayons

Instructions:

1. Choose a text or passage that contains some images or is set in a scene. For example, Psalm 23 or Matthew 6:28, 29.

2. Create a word picture of the verse using all the words in the memory verse, shaping them, coloring them, decorating them, and swirling them on the page to suit the meaning of the verse. Add pictures around the words as you go to illustrate the verse. For example, you might write "consider the lilies of the field" in various colors, drawing lilies by the word "lilies" and curving the end of the phrase down toward a picture of the ground or a field. You could finally add a row of clothes hanging on a line to illustrate how God provides for our clothing needs.

3. Create a sample to show the children what they might do, and then let them write out the verse, changing the shapes and colors of words and adding pictures to illustrate the text in whatever way they like.

Please note: This activity involves some thoughtful reflection about the text and its meaning instead of just copying the words.

Other ideas:

- Create a tiny illustrated accordion book of the verse.
- Frame the verses and make a display in a special area at church.
- Encourage children to create a scrapbook of their word pictures or scan the children's work into a computer and use the illustrated verses as part of a worship experience.

12. Jigsaw Verse

Use with any verse, especially ones that suggest a pictorial image.

Supplies:

- computer with graphics program or patterned cards and markers
- scissors
- poster board
- glue
- envelopes

Instructions:

1. Create an attractive image on your computer that goes along with the theme of the verse you have chosen. Type the words over the image.
2. Print the picture and words onto thin card stock paper, or write the verse with markers on an attractively patterned card.
3. Make one image for each child.
4. Cut up the verse to make a jigsaw puzzle, using traditional jigsaw shaped pieces.
5. Put each verse jigsaw in a different envelope so that they don't get mixed up, or print them on different colored paper.
6. Give one envelope to each child, and let them put the jigsaw puzzle back together again. They can keep their verse as a jigsaw and reuse it, or they can glue their completed jigsaw onto a piece of paper to preserve it.

Other ideas:

- Purchase blank jigsaw puzzles on which you can write your own verse. These will fit together snugly and be more professional. Some craft cutting systems have dies that will quickly cut a small, simple jigsaw for you.
- Create a design on your computer that can be taken to a printer and professionally printed and cut as a jigsaw. Look for this photographic service in your local photo store or on the Internet. This would be unique if a verse is special to your family or group.

- Make picture puzzle blocks. Find 12 plastic or wooden cubes. Choose six verses and print each one on an appropriate picture background. Size the pictures so they can be cut into 12 equal squares that match the size of one side of the cube. Stick one square from each verse onto one side of each of the cubes. Continue until all the verses have been cut and stuck on cubes and each cube has a square from each of the verses stuck onto its sides. Give the children the cubes to rearrange into the different verses.

13. Disappearing Verse

*Use with verses about things that
are hidden or lost.*

Supplies:

- two sheets of thin card stock or strong paper per child
- scissors and/or craft knife and cutting board
- pencils
- markers and crayons
- glue sticks

Instructions:

1. Create a simple design that illustrates the verse to be memorized. Adapt it so that several window flaps can be cut into the design. For example, you can make a design such as a house with windows for the text from Joshua 24:15: "As for me and my household, we will serve the Lord."
2. Draw the design, including the window flaps.
3. Cut open the flaps; fold them back; place a piece of paper under the design, matching the edges of the paper; and write your chosen verse on the paper that shows through the windows. Divide the verse up so each window reveals a few words of the verse in the order in which they will be read.
4. Separate the two sheets, and close the flaps. Copy one design sheet and one verse sheet for each child. Give each child the top design to color.
5. Cut the window flaps after the child has colored the picture. Fold the window flaps so they can be opened and closed. Stick the design with the cut flaps onto a copy of the sheet that has the verse written on it.
6. Have the child open all the flaps and read the complete verse. Then have him shut a flap and say the verse again. When he can say the verse without help, shut another flap and encourage him to say the verse again. Repeat this until all the windows are shut and the child has learned to say the verse all by himself.

Other ideas:

- Write the verse on a chalkboard, whiteboard, or overhead projector so that all the children can see the verse and read it out loud. Wipe off a few words at a time and have the children repeat the verse until all the words have disappeared.
- Write each word on a card, lay the cards in order, and remove a few cards at a time until the children can say the text without any visual prompts.

14. secret codes

Use with any verse.

supplies:

- pencil and paper
- a book of simple secret codes or cryptology (you can also visit the following Web site: www.britishcouncil.org/kids-print-codes.pdf)

instructions:

1. Use the ideas in the secret codebook to create a coded verse for the children to unravel. Or write the first letter of each word in the verse, and use it as a prompt to help the children remember the verse. You can use some fun toy letter shapes or card letters and arrange them in the right order to create the code. For example, "For God so loved the world" would become "fgsltw." Alternatively, another code could use the first two letters of each word; divide them after every six letters and you will get "fogoso lothwo."
2. Give the children some simple clues to help them crack the code, if necessary.

other ideas:

- Help older children to devise a simple code of their own and create coded verses for other children to guess.
- Create and print a small book of coded verses created by the children in your class for other children to decode.
- Create a simple coded verse each week and leave it in the classroom or on a chalkboard at home, and see who can decipher it first.

15. Newspaper Verse

*Use with verses about the Word of God
or the good news of God's love.*

Supplies:

- a pile of newspapers and magazines (make sure they do not contain unsuitable material)
- glue
- scissors
- poster board
- copies of the verses to be created

Instructions:

1. Give each child a copy of the memory verse, a few newspapers, glue, scissors, and a sheet of thin card stock.
2. Have the children search through the papers to find the words they need to create their verse. If words can't be found, individual letters can be cut out to create the words.
3. Glue the cutout words on the poster board in the correct order to make the Bible verse. These can look quite interesting as each word may have a different font style.

Other ideas:

- Cut out pictures from magazines and papers to add to the poster and decorate the verses.
- Have the children work together in groups to find the words they need.

16. crossword/word search puzzles

Use with any verse.

supplies:

- preprinted grid paper
- pencils
- black ink pens
- paper and copier

instructions:

1. Create a word search or a crossword puzzle of all the words in your text. (A word search is a grid full of letters with the different individual words of the text running diagonally, vertically, horizontally, up, down, backward, or forward in the grid, surrounded by other extra letters.) If you are making a crossword puzzle, create an extra square for the single letter words, such as A, I, or O, all on their own. Single letter words are easy to fit into a word search.

2. Convert the references to words so they can be used in the puzzle, too. For example, John three sixteen.

3. Play around with the words until they all fit within the grid if you are creating a crossword puzzle. Then, black out all unused grid spaces and redraw the crossword grid without the words. Make a copy of the empty crossword skeleton and write the full Bible verse on the same page.

4. Fit each word of the verse into the squared grid if you are creating a word search. Overlap words and use letters from one word in another word running in a different direction. Start with the bigger words, and then fit the smaller ones around them. Once you have filled in all the words of the verse, add random letters to all the empty squares in the grid so you have a grid in which each square contains a different letter. Write out the verse and its reference beneath the grid so the children know which words they are looking for.

5. Copy one crossword puzzle or word search per child.

6. Provide pencils or pens for the children to use in completing the puzzles, which should be done by fitting the words of the verse into the crossword skeleton or by circling the words they discover in the word search.

Other ideas:

- Give children grid paper and the memory verse, and let them create their own crossword and word search puzzles. Copy a set of these puzzles for each child so they become familiar with the text while creating—and solving—the puzzles.
- Use these puzzles in the children's bulletins at church to help them learn verses during the worship service.
- Use a word search or crossword puzzle computer design program, or search the Internet for versions you can use online. A good version will allow you to create a hard copy of a word search or crossword puzzle from the words you supply.

17. Join-the-Dots Verse

Use with any verse that suggests a clearly defined shape or verses about being connected together.

Supplies:

- paper
- pencils
- erasers
- pens
- copier

Instructions:

1. Choose a verse that suggests a simple shape, such as a boat, tree, house, etc. Lightly sketch the shape in pencil on a piece of paper.
2. Count how many words there are in your chosen verse, and place the same number of dots around the outline you have drawn. Then, instead of numbering the dots in the usual manner to create a dot-to-dot picture, write the words of the verse in order next to each dot.
3. Check that your dot-to-dot design works. Then, write the words and dots in ink and erase your pencil marks. Copy the design to be sure that you have enough for each child.
4. Practice the memory verse together. Then, give each child a copy of the dot-to-dot activity to reinforce the verse.

Other ideas:

- Show the children how you created the join-the-dots verse design and invite them to try creating their own design for different verses. Perhaps you could find someone who would convert the children's designs into a simple dot-to-dot verse book to help them learn different verses. Include the Bible text and version on each picture so the children can look up the verse to help them, if necessary.

18. Calligraphic Verse

*Use with verses that talk about the beauty
and importance of God's Word.*

Supplies:

- samples of calligraphy and other ornamental lettering from the Internet, greetings cards, books, etc.
- lettering stencils (optional)
- a range of pens with colored inks and different nibs
- pencils and rulers
- scrap paper
- good quality writing paper, perhaps with various textured finishes

Instructions:

1. Show the children some samples of calligraphy so they can see how beautiful good lettering can look. Discuss how the artist might have created the lettering and the design.
2. Give the children a verse to write and some scrap paper to experiment with. Let them know that their verse will be very different from the samples they have seen but that it will still be special and unique because it will be their personal design.
3. Let the children use the pens and paper to create their own calligraphic text when they are happy with the design they created on the scrap paper.

Other ideas:

- Provide simple frames from a budget store so each verse can be specially presented and displayed.
- Use fancy fonts on a computer to create beautiful letters in different colors.
- Use a computer to write out the verse you are using in hollow or outlined letters for younger children to color in. Show them how they can shade the colors they use to make the words look extra special.

- Use the children's work as bulletin covers or pictures around the home or church, or have them scanned into a computer and printed to make larger posters. These verses could also be incorporated into PowerPoint presentations.
- Find out how the verse would look in Chinese or Japanese "lettering," and find someone to teach the children how to create these beautiful symbols. You can also search for these designs on the Internet and print them out to show the children.
- Let the children create a background by writing the verse with different colored pens, overlapping and at different angles, all over a piece of paper. The repeated writing helps them remember the verse. Mount the paper on a colored piece of paper, and let each child choose a simple motif that illustrates the verse to stick in the middle of the background.

19. Mini Book Verse

*Use with verses about the Word of God
or for passages of Scripture that tell a story.*

Supplies:

- paper
- stapler
- pens and markers
- scissors
- craft materials, stickers, foam shapes, etc.

Instructions:

1. Find out how to make different mini books from the Internet or a children's craft book. Books can be made in an accordion format, in which a long strip of paper is folded back and forth to create a series of same sized pages, or in a more traditional page format with rectangles of paper folded in half

2. Draw a simple pattern for the pages of the book, and help the children cut out the design and fasten them together with staples. If the book isn't too thick, it may be easier to staple some sheets of paper together, fold them into a book, and then cut out the book shape through all the layers so that all the pages are the same shape and size.

3. Supply different shapes and materials to decorate the book cover, such as craft foam, felt, recycled denim, thin wood, craft foil, stickers, stick on jewels, etc.

4. Let the children write the verse in the book after the cover of the book has been decorated. Have them write a few words on each page, adding pictures to illustrate the text.

Other ideas:

- Give the children small, inexpensive photo or scrapbook albums, and help them make simple cards of decorated Bible verses to slide into the clear photo sleeves.

20. Verse Response

Use with most verses.

Supplies:

- paper and pens
- crayons, markers, and other craft materials

Instructions:

1. Give each child a piece of paper and a pen.
2. Read the memory verse aloud; then discuss it together. What does it mean? How does it apply to your life today? What does the verse tell us about God's love? If you were to rewrite the text, what would you write? What is the best thing that the verse has to say? What does it say to you personally?
3. Give the children the time and space to write a letter to God in response to the verse after they have explored the verse and what it means.

Other ideas:

- Invite the children to write a poem, song, or story instead of a letter.
- Let them draw a picture or create something instead of writing a reply.

Ten Ways to Learn Memory Verses Using Art Activities

21. Verse Poster
22. Rebus Verse
23. Cartoon Verse
24. Waxresist Verse
25. Postcard Verse
26. Glue Art
27. Verse Mobile
28. Balloon Verse
29. Stained Glass Window Verse
30. Verse Diorama

21. verse poster

Use with any verse.

supplies:

- art supplies
- pencils, rulers, and erasers
- word stencils
- precut paper letters
- large pieces of strong paper

instructions:

1. Give each child a large piece of paper and a copy of the verse to be memorized.
2. Ask them to create a poster to illustrate the verse in any way they like. Show them how to make letters for a poster using the stencils, precut paper letters, or a pencil and a ruler.
3. Let the children have the time and space to create their poster.
4. Display the finished posters.

other ideas:

- Use the posters to make a display in your church.
- Use a clip frame in a prominent place in the church building, and change the poster each week until every child has had their poster displayed. You might like to add the child's photo and a few lines about them so the church members get to know the children in your church better.
- Invite a skilled graphic artist in your church to work with the children and teach them how to design a good poster.

22. Rebus Verse

Use with verses that contain several object words.

Supplies:

- plain paper
- pencils
- pens and markers
- a variety of sticker sheets or printed clip art to suit the text being illustrated

Instructions:

1. Create a Rebus by replacing some of the words in the verse with pictures. This activity is useful for early and prereaders because the pictures help the children to guess some of the words. Choose verses containing several words for which you can find replacement pictures or stickers.
2. Help the children to write out the verse to be learned, leaving spaces for small pictures where appropriate.
3. Let the children place stickers or small pictures into the correct spaces in the verse.

Other ideas:

- Help younger children by preprinting the verse with ready made spaces for the stickers and pictures, and give each of them a copy.
- Make a series of Rebus verses and let each child build up a small folder or booklet of Rebus verses that they can reread whenever they wish.
- Have older children draw their own pictures in the spaces.

23. cartoon verse

Use with verses from Proverbs and parables.

supplies:

- paper and pencils
- rulers
- crayons

Instructions:

1. Show the children some examples of good cartoons. You may have a book of Bible cartoons you can show them, or you can search the Internet for appropriate cartoons.
2. Look at what makes a good cartoon, including single frame cartoons and a comic strip format.
3. Give them the Bible verse and ask them to create a cartoon of the verse. The book of Proverbs is a rich source for verses that can inspire cartoons. Some of the shorter parables of Jesus can also be used.
4. Show them how to plan their cartoon on scrap paper first. Help them plan how many scenes they will need and what they will write or draw on each one.
5. Collect the finished cartoons, and create a display.

Other ideas:

- Give the children a copy of all the verses in one chapter of Proverbs, and let them choose which verse to illustrate and learn.
- Print good cartoons in your church magazine or newsletter.

24. waxresist verse

*Use with verses about color, rainbows,
or hidden things becoming visible.*

supplies:

- thin white candles or white wax crayons
- slightly diluted water based washable paints in different colors
- water
- large paintbrushes
- large sheets of paper
- protection for tables, floors, and clothes during the painting

instructions:

1. Write the verse clearly using the candle or white wax crayon on the large sheet of paper. Write one copy of the verse per sheet until you have one copy for each child.
2. Give each child a piece of paper with the verse written on it. The verse should be almost invisible to the child.
3. Give each child a large paintbrush and access to a variety of paint colors.
4. Ask each child to fill their paper with their favorite paint colors. As they paint, the colors will cover the paper except for the places where the wax verse has been written, and the white words will show through the paint.
5. Let each child read their verse and talk about what the verse means after it has been revealed.

other ideas:

- Add simple pictures to the paper using the white wax, such as hearts and smiley faces.
- Let the children write out their own verse with the wax, and then have them paint over the paper.

- Show the children how to write short Bible verses on fabric, using a special batik tool and wax (if you are skilled with batik), and then use cold water dye to color the fabric. Once the fabric has been dyed, the wax can be removed by placing several layers of kitchen paper over the wax and ironing with a hot iron. When all the wax has been absorbed by the paper, the fabric can be ironed to fix the dye. The fabric verses can then be made into pillows, or a selection of different promises can be stitched together to make a quilt to give to someone in need of encouragement. Add buttons, lace, and other embellishments to enhance the design.
- Write the verse on white paper with an old pen that doesn't have any ink left in it. Place a few sheets of newsprint under the paper so the invisible writing makes an impression on the paper but the paper still looks blank. Give the verse to the child, and let them rub over it softly using the unwrapped side of a wax crayon or a colored pencil, rubbing gently in the same direction each time. The verse should appear in white as they color.

25. postcard verse

Use with encouraging promises.

Supplies:

- blank postcards
- samples of postcards that have words and artwork on them
- art and craft supplies, especially ones that will work well with the theme of the verse
- pencils, erasers, scissors, and glue
- clear card protection sleeves—like the ones that protect some purchased cards—available from good craft stores

Instructions:

1. Give each child a blank postcard and a copy of the Bible verse to be learned.
2. Invite each child to think about how the Bible verse could be illustrated.
3. Provide the children with a selection of craft and art materials to create an attractive postcard of their verse.
4. Bring all the cards together and let the children see each other's work. Read the Bible verses.
5. Protect the children's work by slipping the cards into the clear protective sleeves.

Other ideas:

- Invite the children to write a short message on their postcard and send it to someone, if they wish. If the children want to keep their own cards, perhaps they could mail their card to a family member, so they can keep it after it has been received.
- Supply the names and addresses of church members and others who might appreciate an encouraging card.

- Prepare the postcards for mailing by writing the address on it and inserting it in a clear protective sleeve before adding the postage stamp. This process should be followed for postcards with collages that need to be protected for mailing.
- Make a display board of the postcards.
- Scan the finished cards so they can be reproduced. Perhaps some of the cards could be printed and sold to raise funds for a special project.

26. Glue art

Use with verses about seeds, flowers, sand, etc.

Supplies:

- a large piece of colored poster board for each child
- pencils and erasers
- thick glue in small easy-to-squeeze containers
- wet wipes to mop up excess glue and correct mistakes
- glitter or colored sand
- protection for clothes, tables, and floor

Instructions:

1. Write the Bible verse in clear letters on the poster board. Older children can manage this for themselves. Use pencils so mistakes can be erased.
2. Give each child a bottle of glue and show them how to squeeze the glue carefully over the pencil letters as if they were writing with the glue.
3. Leave the glue to dry a little so it won't run and drip, and then let the children sprinkle glitter or colored sand over their words.
4. Leave the letters for a few more moments and then pour the excess glitter or sand into a pot so it can be used another time. If the children are using a variety of colors, let them use one color at a time over different sections of the verse so the excess can be collected as separate colors and reused.
5. Let the whole verse dry completely before moving it.

Other ideas:

- Add beads, pressed flowers, or other items that suit the theme of the text.
- Use seeds, such as alfalfa seeds, instead of glitter or sand for texts that talk about seeds. If you use seeds, be mindful of children with seed and nut allergies and do not use any seeds that could be harmful to the children.

27. verse mobile

*Use with verses about being connected to God
or about the Holy Spirit moving like the wind.*

supplies:

- pieces of colored, patterned, and white card stock
- scrap paper
- pencils
- markers
- hole punch
- glue
- scissors
- colored yarn
- wire coat hangers
- craft supplies

instructions:

1. Give each child a wire coat hanger and a copy of the Bible verse to be learned.
2. Give them a scrap of paper so they can design a mobile of their verse. They can then cut shapes out of the card stock to suit the theme of the verse and write a few words of the verse on each shape.
3. Punch holes in the shapes so they can be hung in order from the hanger using the colored yarn.
4. Decorate the mobile with craft supplies.
5. Encourage the children to hang the completed mobiles in their bedroom to help them learn the verse.

other ideas:

- Hang additional shapes from the bottom of the shapes that have the words written on them. Perhaps you can hang a bird, star, or heart, etc., depending on the verse being learned.
- Use large precut foam shapes instead of card stock.

28. Balloon Verse

Use with verses of praise, verses about the Holy Spirit, or verses that can be illustrated with balloon shapes.

Supplies:

- a sturdy, plain colored balloon for each child, tied to a string or ribbon or fastened to a balloon stick
- permanent markers
- scraps of craft materials, colored card stock and paper, etc.
- double sided tape
- scissors

Instructions:

1. Give each child a copy of the verse to be learned.
2. Let them use the markers to write the verse on the balloon.
3. Decorate the balloon to suit the passage. Craft items, card shapes, folded paper, and curled ribbons can be added to the balloon to illustrate the verse.
4. Give each child an opportunity to say the verse out loud and show his or her balloon.

Other ideas:

- Use mylar balloons since they are strong and often stay inflated for several weeks.
- Use heart shaped balloons for verses about love.
- Transform long balloons into butterflies by attaching cellophane wings. This will work for verses like 2 Corinthians 5:17 that talk about becoming a new creation.
- Use oval and round balloons to make faces and people.

29. Stained glass window verse

Use with verses about light and seeing.

Supplies:

- sheets of overhead transparency acetate
- copier and paper
- a simple stained glass window outline printed on paper
- masking tape
- permanent overhead projector pens, glass painting pens, or paints
- glass outliner paint (optional)
- double sided tape to stick the verse to a window

Instructions:

1. Create a simple pattern for a stained glass window, and draw it on a piece of paper.
2. Add the Bible verse centered at the bottom of the window.
3. Make enough copies for one pattern per child.
4. Give each child a copy of the pattern and a sheet of acetate.
5. Help each child stick their sheet of acetate to their pattern paper using a few small pieces of masking tape.
6. Let each child color in sections of the window with the overhead projector pens (available in a variety of bright colors from a graphics store). When the background has been filled in, let each child write the memory verse in black, and outline the window shapes with black pen or outliner paint.
7. Leave the stained glass pictures to dry, and then remove the masking tape.
8. Stick the pictures to a window using the double sided tape.

Other ideas:

- Create a stained glass effect by printing the window pattern and memory verse on strong tracing paper and letting the children color the design with markers.

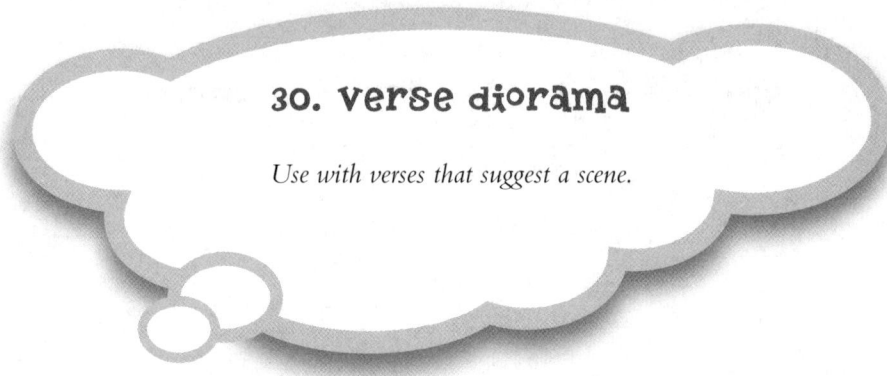

30. verse diorama

Use with verses that suggest a scene.

supplies:

- one sturdy shoe box per child (discard the lid)
- strong plain paper to cover the outside of the shoe box
- scissors
- strong glue or double sided tape
- pencils
- crayons and markers
- poster board scraps
- wired chenille sticks
- craft foam
- a variety of other craft materials depending on the verse being learned and created

instructions:

1. Cover the outside of each shoe box with plain paper.
2. Give each child a box and a copy of the verse to be learned.
3. Let the children write the Bible verse along one of the long sides so the open box can lie on its other long side and become a shadow box.
4. Show the children how to make people, animals, and buildings out of poster board by drawing shapes, adding tabs at the base of the shape, and cutting them out. Stick the shapes by the tabs onto the floor of the box.
5. Let them create a scene to illustrate the verse using craft materials to create the scenery and other items for their three dimensional diorama.

other ideas:

- Give each child a different verse from a longer passage of Scripture (such as Psalm 23), and let each make a different scene. Display them in sequence and help the children say the verses as they look at each of the displays.
- Supply items such as a small mirror for still water, a cup that can overflow, a toy table, etc.

Ten Ways to Learn Memory Verses Using Crafts

31. Key Ring Verse
32. Clay Plaque
33. Verse Clock
34. Bible Bookmarks
35. Promise Box
36. Verse Planter
37. Verse Scrapbook
38. Lantern Verse
39. Magnetic Verse
40. Pocket Verse

31. Key ring verse

Use with any verse that has several clearly identifiable objects in it.

Supplies:

- one plain key ring per child
- a variety of different buttons and beads to suit the items needed by the verse (these can be found in good craft stores)
- alphabet beads
- strong bead thread, jute thread, or wire
- wax candle and matches (use with care)

Instructions:

1. Choose buttons and beads that illustrate the verse to be learned. You can use alphabet beads as prompts for words by using the initial letters of key words.
2. Talk about the verse and let the children help you choose the buttons and beads they need to form the verse.
3. Line up the buttons and beads in the order in which they are needed for the verse. For example, Galatians 5:22, 23 says, "But the fruit of the Spirit is love, joy, peace, patience, kindness, goodness, faithfulness, gentleness and self-control." For this verse you could use the following buttons/beads: fruit, heart (love), smiley face (joy), dove (peace), thimble (patience), flower (kindness), apple (goodness), Bible, cross, praying hands, or church (faithfulness), butterfly (gentleness), lemon (self-control), or use letter beads for the first letter of the key words: B F S L J P P K G F G S.
4. Give the children a length of strong thread so they can thread the beads and buttons in the correct order. Dip the end of the thread in melted candle wax to make it stiff enough to easily push through the holes.
5. Loop the thread around and fasten it to the key ring, or use the method suggested on the instructions for using the key rings you have bought.

6. Show the children how to use the shaped beads as prompts to help them remember the verse they have threaded together.

other ideas:

- Show the girls how to use the key ring as a bag charm, clipping it decoratively onto their school bag, purse, or jeans belt loops.
- Use clear acrylic key rings, and let the children write the Bible verse on the small card shapes that fit into the acrylic tags.

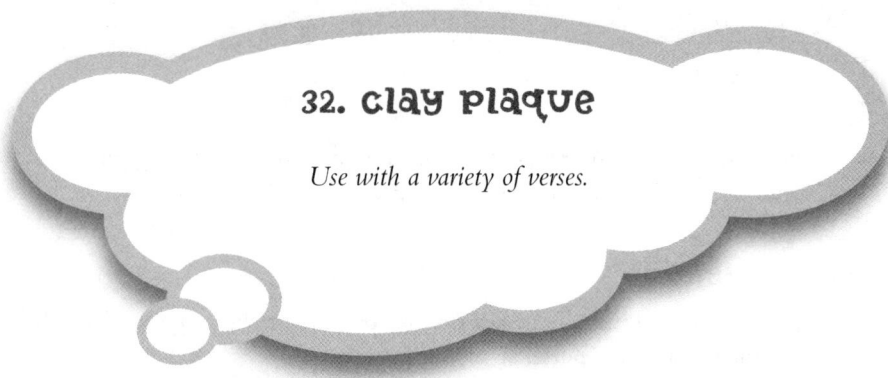

32. Clay Plaque

Use with a variety of verses.

Supplies:

- air-drying clay or oven baked clay
- rolling pins or lengths of dowel
- modeling sticks, sharpened narrow dowels, or pencils
- textured objects that can be pressed into the clay, such as keys, grasses, flat leaves with interesting undersides, craft stamps, burlap, etc.
- small pastry, cookie, or sugar craft cutters
- drinking straws
- paints suitable for the clay
- brushes
- clear protective finish
- lengths of ribbon for hanging

Instructions:

1. Give the children a ball of clay to roll out into a plaque of any shape they want. You or the children can use the small pointed sticks to write the words of the verse into the clay. Mistakes can easily be corrected by rerolling the clay.
2. Let the children press different objects into the clay, removing them to leave an indented shape. Use things that illustrate the verse where possible. Even the underside of fresh leaves can make interesting patterns on the clay. Cutters can be used to press out tiny shapes that can be attached to their plaque. Alternatively, objects such as flowers, sheep, etc., can be molded from the clay to decorate their work.
3. Use a drinking straw to make a couple of holes near the top edge so a length of ribbon can be threaded through to hang the plaque.
4. Let the plaques dry or bake them according to the instructions provided with the clay.
5. Have the children paint their work once the plaques dry. It should then be finished with a sealing varnish.

6. Thread ribbon through the holes for hanging.

other ideas:

- Press small (child and allergy safe) seeds and other tiny objects into the plaque, and leave them in the clay to create a design. If the clay is to be baked, use items that will be safe in the oven.
- Give each child a plain white wall tile, and use special ceramic paint pens that become permanent when they have been baked in an oven. They can write their verse and decorate the tile with the colored pens. Follow the instructions on the pens for baking the tiles. If the children make a variety of tiles with different verses, these could be used on the wall around a sink in the church. Or the tiles can be backed with protective felt to become pot stands to use at home. To hang a tile on the wall as a plaque, attach a hanger to the back with strong glue.

33. Verse Clock

Use with verses about time.

Supplies:

- one flat, blank wooden clock face per child (look for this item at your local craft store)
- one clock mechanism per child, plus batteries
- adhesive clock numbers (optional)
- plastic or poster board to make a template
- thin card stock
- pencils and erasers
- markers
- stickers, stencils, etc.
- scissors
- putty adhesive
- hole punch
- copies of the memory verse to be learned
- laminator (optional)

Instructions:

1. Make a template for the face of the clock you have chosen to use, allowing space for the numbers if you plan to use them.
2. Give the children a piece of thin card stock and ask them to draw around the clock face template and cut out the shape. Punch a hole in the center of the card stock for the hand mechanism to pass through.
3. Invite them to write the memory verse in an attractive way on the card stock. Let them decorate the face with any flat embellishments, such as stickers, stencils, etc.
4. Laminate the decorated clock face if you wish, repunching the hole for the hands, if necessary.

5. Assemble the clock with any numbers you wish to use, then the clock face, and finally the hands and the battery mechanism. You can stick the clock face down permanently or use putty adhesive if you want to change the design.
6. Tell the children to place the clock where they will see it often and become familiar with the verse.

other ideas:

- Let the children make a series of clock faces for different verses so they can change them regularly.

34. Bible bookmarks

Use with any verse.

Supplies:

- ribbons
- beads
- paper
- markers
- envelopes
- pencil and ruler

Instructions:

Ribbon bookmark

1. Make a special verse finder bookmark using several 60 cm. (2 ft.) lengths of different colored narrow ribbon.
2. Thread all the ribbons through the hole of a large bead and move the bead to the center of the ribbons.
3. Tie all the ribbons together beneath the bead in a double flat knot (reef or square knot), and slide a tightly fitting bead over the knot. The ribbons can then be used to mark several verses throughout the Bible. The colors of the ribbons can help to identify the verses, or numbered beads can be attached to the free ends of the ribbons so that verses can be located in a specific sequence for a Bible study, for example.

Fish bookmark

1. Fold a piece of paper in half along its length and cut out the shape of a fish.
2. Make a series of parallel, short, evenly spaced diagonal cuts along its body.
3. Cut from the fold toward the tail, leaving a strong border around the edge.
4. Open the fish, and you will have V-shaped cuts.
5. Fold the V's back to create a pattern of scales. This looks even better when the paper has a different color on each side.

6. Write the text on the edge of the body, or write one word on each folded scale.

Triangular bookmark

1. Use colored envelopes, and seal the flap of the envelope.

2. Make a mark 7 cm. (3 in.) from the corner of the envelope, along the top and side of the envelope.

3. Join these two marks with a pencil and ruler to create a triangular corner shape.

4. Cut along the pencil line, and use this triangle to slip over the corner of the page.

Other ideas:

- Make bookmarks from strips of card stock and decorate them with lettering and stickers or other suitable flat items. The bookmarks can be laminated to make them durable and glossy. Choose bookmark shapes that suit the verse to be learned. More ideas can be found in paper craft books, hobby stores, and on the Internet.
- Decorate the triangle shapes to suit the verse.
- Hold a bookmark exhibition or competition. Show children samples of purchased and handmade bookmarks, and invite them to create a special bookmark of their favorite verse. Display these at church and give prizes for creativity, or reward each child with their choice of one of the purchased bookmarks.
- Hold a bookmark auction as a fundraising event, selling any bookmarks the children are willing to part with.
- Organize a bookmark exchange. Give each child a different verse and ask them to make a bookmark of their verse. When they are done, hold a swap session so everyone gets a collection of verse bookmarks to place in their Bible.

35. promise box

Use with a variety of verses.

supplies:

- small purchased gift boxes
- precut cards, such as blank business cards, that fit in the box
- pens and markers
- list of Bible promises
- a collection of items to decorate the boxes

Instructions:

1. Give the children a list of the Bible texts, pens, a gift box, and a stack of blank cards.
2. Let them look up the texts and copy each verse and its reference onto a different card.
3. Put the cards into the boxes, and decorate the boxes.

other ideas:

- Add new cards to the box each week after new verses have been learned.
- Use another type of container, such as a pocket cut from an old pair of jeans, a small basket, a gift bag, etc.
- Use a clear, vinyl pouch, like those used to create conference name tags, and stick a small piece of adhesive magnet onto the back of the pouch to create a fridge magnet. The promise verses can then be slotted into the pouch and displayed on the fridge so they can be learned.

36. Verse Planter

Use with verses about growing and planting.

Supplies:

- plain terracotta pots
- acrylic craft paint
- pencils
- paper
- paintbrushes (wide for coverage and fine for detail)
- protection for clothes, table, and floor

Instructions:

1. Choose a verse about fruit, flowers, growing, etc.
2. Give each child a terracotta pot and the brushes and paint. To save time, you may want to paint the pots before giving them to the children.
3. Paint the pot a base coat of paint. The pot may need two coats for good coverage.
4. Give the children paper, pencils, and the verse to be painted on the pot. Invite them to create a design for the pot that includes the Bible verse. Planning the design on paper ensures that it will fit well on the pot.
5. Transfer the child's design onto the pot using a pencil. Then, paint the design with the paints and fine brushes.

Other ideas:

- Use permanent ink pens to write the verse on the pot as an alternative to the fine brushes.
- Plant seeds or flowers in the finished pot for the child to take home. Perhaps a Bible verse could be chosen that would be a good text for Mothers' Day or for someone who is ill. The finished pot could then be given as a gift.

37. verse scrapbook

Use with longer passages of scripture.

supplies:

- a scrapbook, folder, or album with pages
- craft scraps of all kinds suitable for the verses to be learned
- paper clips
- scissors
- pens
- markers
- glue

instructions:

1. Let each child write one verse of the passage on a different piece of scrap paper. Clip the verses, in order, to different pages in the scrapbook or album.
2. Encourage the children to think about what the verse means to them and how they would like to illustrate the different verses. As they gather scraps and ideas, help them to think about how they would like to write the verses in the scrapbook and arrange their chosen items on each page. The children might like to add other words to each page, as they think about the ideas they have about the verses.
3. Provide all kinds of materials to help the children decorate each page.

other ideas:

- Lend or give the scrapbooks to people who are housebound or in the hospital.

38. Lantern Verse

*Use with verses about light,
witnessing, food, or celebration.*

Supplies:

- one small glass jar per person with a neck wide enough to pass a tealight through
- one flat plate per person
- a large sheet of firm translucent paper, such as parchment
- double sided tape
- glue
- star sequins
- gold ink pens
- salt crystals
- tealight and matches or a battery operated tealight

Instructions:

1. Cut a long strip of parchment paper about 8 cm. (5 in.) wide.
2. Wrap the paper around in a circle about 2 cm. (1 in.) wider than the jar. Add a small flap about 1 cm. (½ in.).
3. Measure the length of the paper, minus the flap, and divide it by five. Mark the parchment length into five separate sections, and make a fold along the edge of each section.
4. Give each child a gold pen to write the Bible verse on the parchment.
5. Decorate the lantern with gold stars or other suitable shapes by gluing the shapes to the parchment paper.
6. Use double sided tape to stick the edges of the strip together, creating a five-sided paper lantern.
7. Place the paper lantern on a plate.

8. Fill the bottom of the jar with salt crystals. Carefully add a lit tealight or battery operated candle to the jar, and then place the jar inside the paper lantern.

Other ideas:

- Use glass painting outliner paint to write a short Bible verse on a clean glass jar, and decorate the jar with glass paints to create a glass lantern.
- Use special oven bake markers for permanently decorating ceramics. Use the markers to write and illustrate Bible verses on flat plates, dishes, mugs, or any other crockery. Words can be matched to the items—verses about water and drinking can be written on mugs; verses about food and God's provision can be written on plates.

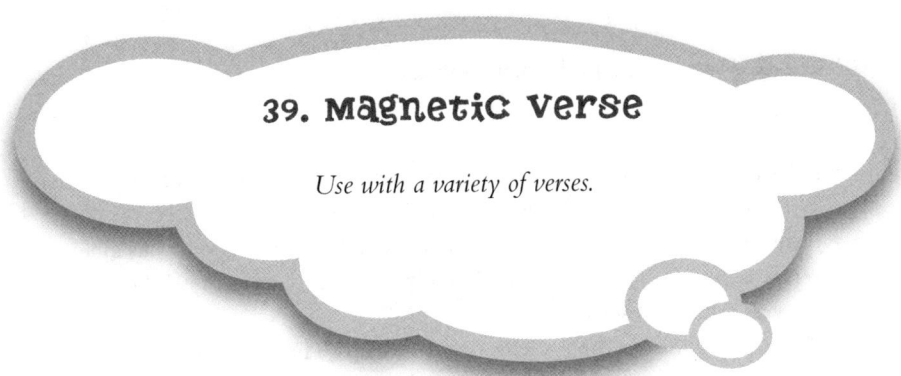

39. Magnetic Verse

Use with a variety of verses.

Supplies:

- thin card stock that will go through a computer printer
- computer and printer
- scissors or paper cutter
- laminator and laminating pouches
- one roll of adhesive magnetic strips
- small envelopes

Instructions:

1. Choose a clear font on your computer and a size that is easy for children to read.
2. Type the words of the chosen text, with plenty of space around each word.
3. Print the words onto thin card stock. Laminate the card and use a paper cutter to neatly separate the words.
4. Stick a small amount of magnetic tape onto the back of each laminated word.
5. Put each set of Bible verse magnets in a different envelope.
6. Give each child a set of magnetic words to rearrange into the Bible verse. A clean metal cookie sheet can be used as a base for the words while the child is putting the memory verse together.
7. Place the magnetic words on the fridge at home to help the children learn the memory verse.

Other ideas:

- Purchase white magnetic sheets that can run through a computer printer and be cut to size.

- Print lots of extra words to create a magnetic Bible verse kit. The words can be used to create different Bible verses from week to week.
- Print some pictures as well as words so the children can create Rebus memory verses, where some words are replaced by pictures to help the children 'read' the verses for themselves.
- Write and illustrate Bible verses on small cards. These can be laminated and made into fridge magnets by sticking adhesive magnet strip on their backs.
- Purchase a children's magnetic poetry kit to give you lots of words to get started with, and add other words as needed.

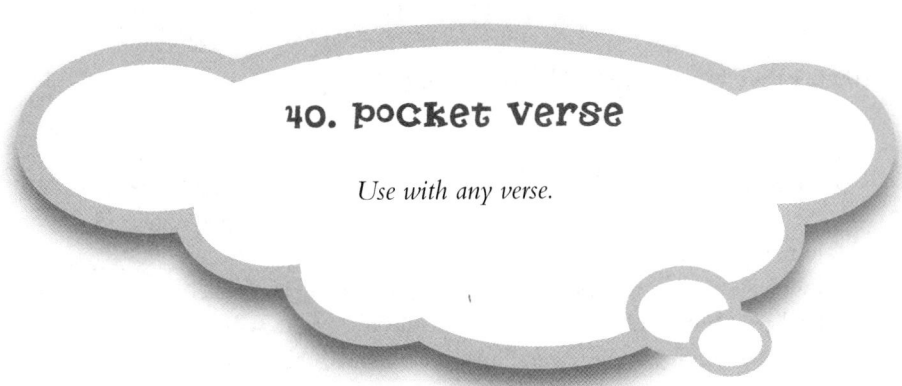

40. pocket verse

Use with any verse.

supplies:

- clear vinyl, purchased from a fabric store
- clear nylon thread or white thread
- scissors
- ruler
- water soluble overhead projector pens
- thin card stock
- markers
- an assortment of items related to the Bible verse
- glitter, metallic confetti, etc.

instructions:

1. Sew a small, simple square or rectangular tote bag out of the clear vinyl with four clear vinyl pockets on one side. Make one for each child.
2. Give each child a piece of thin card stock, cut to a size that will easily fit into the pockets.
3. Have the children write the memory verse and illustrate it. Slide the card into one of the pockets. Add several items that illustrate the text to the other clear pockets to create a contemporary and interesting display.
4. Close the pocket by stitching across the opening or sealing with double sided tape, if you want to make a permanent display. Or leave open some pockets so objects can be easily changed.

other ideas:

- Encourage the children to use the bag to carry items to church.

- Give each child a small stack of cards that they can write and illustrate on so they can change the verse on display in their bag, as well as the items that illustrate the text.
- Purchase clear vinyl purses, pencil cases, or photo display hangers with multiple pockets. Or use individual clear vinyl collectors' pages with pockets designed to display photos or postcards. These alternatives can be used if you don't want to make clear tote bags.

Ten Ways to Learn Memory Verses Using Paper

41. Verse Flower
42. Verse Crown
43. Origami Verse
44. Mini Scroll
45. Everlasting Strip
46. Paper Word Cutouts
47. Verse Loops
48. Layered Booklet
49. Paper Chain Verse
50. Accordion Pleated Booklets

41. Verse Flower

Use with verses about flowers and plants.

Supplies:

- paper in a variety of bright colors
- glue sticks
- scissors
- pens

Instructions:

1. Use one piece of colored paper for the background of the flower.
2. Cut out a big oval shaped petal for each word or short phrase of the verse to be learned.
3. Arrange the petals in word order to make a circular flower shape with the petals radiating out from the central point.
4. Cut a circle to fit in the center of the flower and stick it over the central edges of the petals. Write the Bible text on this shape.
5. Add a narrow green paper stem and leaves.

Other ideas:

- Curve the outer edge of the petals slightly to give a sculptured look to the flower. Another way to add dimension to the picture is to fold the leaves in half and open them out again before sticking them onto the background paper.
- Explore books of simple flower patterns to create different styles and shapes.
- Use precut paper flower shapes and write one word on each flower. Arrange them on the paper to make a garden, planter, or bouquet, making sure they are stuck down in word order.
- Make large paper tree pictures, and write the words on fruit or leaf shapes that can be stuck onto the tree in verse order.

42. verse Crown

*Use with verses about our thoughts,
kings, victory, and salvation.*

supplies:

- a strip of gold card stock that is wide and long enough to make a crown for a child's head
- scissors
- stapler and staples
- tape
- glue sticks
- bright stickers or gummed paper shapes
- pens

Instructions:

1. Cut the card stock into a crown shape, slightly longer then the circumference of the child's head.
2. Lay the crown out flat.
3. Write one word of the Bible verse on each sticker or gummed shape.
4. Stick them in word order along the center of the gold strip. Check that the words are well spaced before sticking down.
5. Curve the crown into shape and staple the ends together to make a smooth circular crown.
6. Stick a small piece of tape over the staples on the inside of the crown so they don't scratch the children or catch their hair.
7. Give the crown to the children to wear.

other ideas:

- Add extra decorations to the crown with stick on gems and other embellishments.
- Write one word (or key word, such as in Philippians 4:8—pure, lovely, etc.) of the verse on each crown, and see if the children can arrange themselves into the correct word order.

43. Origami Verse

Use with verses that suit the origami patterns available to you.

Supplies:

- a book of simple origami patterns
- a pack of origami paper
- fine tipped pen

Instructions:

1. Choose a simple origami shape that fits with the verse and the ability of the children learning the verse.
2. Learn how to make it so you can guide the children through every step of the folding process.
3. Encourage accuracy and crisp folds.
4. Write the verse on the finished product so it can be seen easily.

Other ideas:

- Stick the finished shapes into a scrapbook or small album. Alternatively they can be made into mobiles, magnets, cards, and other craft items.

44. Mini Scroll

Use with any verse.

Supplies:

- strips of paper or paper that looks like parchment
- two sticks per person
- pens
- tape

Instructions:

1. Cut the paper so it is in strips that are about 20 cm. (8 in.) long. Ensure that the sticks are longer than the paper is wide.
2. Make a mini scroll by carefully applying glue to each short end of the paper and rolling it around a stick. Hold it carefully in place while the glue dries.
3. Write the verse to be learned on the scroll, and carefully roll the scroll up from both ends. Hold it tight, and smooth the paper around the sticks.
4. Unroll again to read the verse. Talk about how scrolls were made in Bible times and how they would have been used.

Other ideas:

- Give each child a small gold gift box in which they can keep their scrolls, as well as other Bible verse activities.
- Teach the children how to write one of the words in the verse in Hebrew. Some concordances and special Bibles have samples of Hebrew words.

45. Everlasting strip

Use with verses about miracles and God's amazing powers.

Supplies:

- a long strip of paper at least 5 cm. (2 in.) wide
- tape
- pens
- scissors

Instructions:

1. Write the Bible verse along the top half of the strip of paper. Make sure all words are away from the central line of the strip.
2. Lay the strip out flat. Pick up the two ends of the strip, and bring them together to make a circle. Before sticking the circle together, make a half twist in one of the ends of the paper.
3. Stick the two ends of the strip together firmly.
4. Take a pair of scissors, and cut a line along the middle of the strip, all the way around, parallel to the long edge of the strip. When you have finished cutting, instead of having two circles, you will have one very big circle! The circle illustrates the way that eternity goes on forever.

Other ideas:

- Find a book of simple paper tricks, and see if any could be used to enhance the learning of a memory verse.

46. Paper Word Cutouts

Use with any verse.

Supplies:

- copies of the verse to be learned (preferably a shorter verse)
- paper
- pencils
- rulers
- scissors
- graph paper
- craft knives and cutting boards (for adult use)
- large sheets of colored paper for mounting the verse to create a poster

Instructions:

1. Make a sample cutout word by drawing outlines of the letters in a word on a piece of paper, making sure that each letter is connected to its neighboring letter. The goal is to create a single cutout shape that spells a word. Once you are happy with the design, cut it out. Graph paper can help you organize and space the letters.
2. Give each child one or more of the words in the verse, so all the words are distributed between the children, according to their ability.
3. Show the children your sample word and some ideas of how to create a cutout word.
4. Provide each child with a pencil, paper, ruler, scissors, graph paper, etc.
5. Ask the children to make a paper cutout of the words they have been given.
6. Arrange the cutout words to make a verse, and stick them onto a backing sheet.
7. Read the verse together.

other ideas:

- Create outline words for the children to cut out so they do not have to design their words, if you are short on time.
- Give children different colored paper to cut out to create a bright display.
- Invite older children to create a cutout of an entire verse from one sheet of paper. Provide large sheets of strong paper for the children to use to create their cutouts. Adult help may be needed to cut out the words using craft knives and cutting boards. These designs can be mounted on colored paper and framed to create attractive and inspiring artwork.

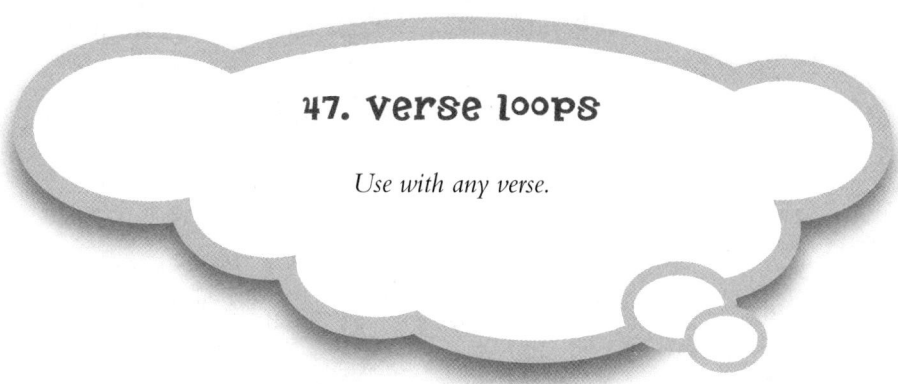

47. verse loops

Use with any verse.

supplies:

- sheets of thin card stock
- scissors and craft knives
- pencils and erasers
- markers

Instructions:

1. Take a sheet of card stock, and place it in landscape orientation with the long sides horizontal.
2. Cut two narrow slots in the card stock, about 3 cm. (1¼ in.) long and 3 mm. (¼ in.) wide, about 3 cm. (1¼ in.) away from the midline of the paper.
3. Write the verse on a strip of card stock that can be cut from one of the long sides of your paper. Allow a small blank space at the end of the verse for an overlap.
4. Thread the strip through the slots from the back so that only a small part of the verse appears on the front of the paper.
5. Fasten the two ends of the strip together with clear tape, making sure the tape covers the front and back edges of the overlap so there are no loose ends to catch on the slots and tear the paper. Children can then slide the word loop around and read the verse from the front of the paper.

other ideas:

- Make a verse wheel out of two circles of card stock fastened together with a brass fastener so the top circle can spin freely. Cut a small window near the edge of the top circle, so you can see the lower circle through the hole. Put your pencil point into one of the bottom corners of the window hole and then spin the top circle so you make a light pencil circle all around the lower circle. Separate the two circles and carefully write your text on the pencil line you have made on the lower circle. Check that the verse fits around this pencil line, and then write over the verse words in ink. Fasten the two circles together again so you can spin the top circle and read the memory verse through the window.

48. Layered Books

Use with a variety of verses.

Supplies:

- strips of white copier paper cut in half from top to bottom so they are long and narrow
- rulers
- pencils
- pens and markers
- long armed stapler and staples, or hole punch and yarn or ribbon

Instructions:

1. Lay one piece of paper on the table. Place the next piece of paper on top, but with the bottom edge 1 cm. (½ in.) up from the bottom edge of the first sheet of paper. Add another layer, again placing it 1 cm. above the edge of the second sheet. Add a fourth layer in the same way so each piece of paper is in a pile with the bottom edges staggered at 1 cm. intervals.
2. Hold the stack of paper firmly and fold the top edge of the pile over, so the top edge of the fourth sheet folds back to 1 cm. above its bottom edge, and the other top edges fold over with 1 cm. intervals. This should give you a booklet that has a fold at the top and eight pages of varying lengths with the shortest page as the top cover and the longest page as the bottom cover. Fasten the booklet pages together with staples, or tie yarn or ribbon through a couple of punched holes.
3. Divide the memory verse into six sections, plus the Bible text.
4. Write one section along the visible edge of each page, leaving the top cover empty. Write the text on the last page.
5. Let the children decorate their book covers to suit the verse. Give the book a title, and write their name on the cover of their book.
6. Have the children draw whatever they like on each page, perhaps drawing pictures to suit that section of the verse.

7. Turn the pages over to hide the previous sections of the verse. The book can be used to help the children learn the Bible verse one section at a time.

other ideas:

- Add extra strips to give the book more layered pages for longer verses.
- Use lined paper to help the children space the pages evenly. You can do this by matching up the bottom edge of each page with a printed line on the previous page.
- Make a larger version from plain wallpaper to help groups learn a verse together. Each page can be illustrated to help the children visualize the verse as they learn the words.
- Have the children make a collection of layered books with different verses written on them. They can then keep them together in a small decorated box.

49. Paper Chain Verse

Use with any verse.

Supplies:

- brightly colored paper (precut self-adhesive paper chain paper can be purchased)
- paper cutter
- double sided tape with a backing strip
- markers
- copies of the verse to be learned

Instructions:

1. Stick a strip of double-sided tape along the edge of one side of the paper. Leave the backing strip in place, and then cut 2 cm. (½ in.) strips across the width of the paper using a paper cutter. This will give you lots of narrow strips of paper with a small piece of tape at one end of the strip.
2. Give each child a selection of different colored strips of paper. They will need one strip for each word in the verse.
3. Ask the children to write one word of the verse on each strip of paper so the word is clearly visible.
4. Make paper chains by taking the first word strip and peeling the backing off the double sided tape and sticking the strip ends together to form a circle. Add the next word by looping the second strip through the first loop before sticking the ends together. Continue adding links until the whole verse is formed.
5. Hang the chain where everyone can see it. You will not be able to see all the words at once, but that doesn't matter. The words you can see will help you remember the ones you can't see.

Other ideas:

- Use a cardboard shape with a narrow slot cut into the shape near the bottom edge. Use a shape that suits the verse, and write the verse and its reference on the cardboard shape. Then let the children attach their first chain link word to this shape, and the next word to the first paper loop and so on. The verse will hang vertically down the wall.
- Give each team a posterboard shape and a set of prewritten word strips. Team members can select a word and then run up to the place where the shapes are hanging and add each link in turn, being sure to get them in the correct order.
- Hide the prewritten paper strips around the room, and let the children find their own set to create their verse chains.
- Use a computer to print pages of one word at a time, spaced and sized to suit the size of the paper strips. Write in the first word of the verse, and set it up so that the spacing is correct. Then use the "find and replace" feature to change all the links to the second word you need, which saves you from having to type each word individually.

50. Accordion Pleated Booklets

Use with a variety of verses.

Supplies:

- large pieces of good quality paper
- scissors
- markers
- pencils, erasers, and rulers
- cardboard or plastic to make templates

Instructions:

1. Think about the Bible verse and choose a shape that suits the content, such as a heart, person, house, tree, etc.
2. Draw a simple template for your shape, and make sure that it has a short straight section on both sides so it can be placed against a fold.
3. Cut a long strip of paper about 8 cm. (3 in.) wide and as long as your paper will allow. If you need a longer piece of paper, tape two pieces together. Fold the paper into an accordion, as wide as your template.
4. Place the template on the folded paper, and trace the outline of your shape. Cut along your outline, taking care to leave sections of folded paper at each side of the shape so the pages hold together.
5. Open the booklet and check that it works.
6. Adjust the template if necessary and then use it to help the children fold and cut booklets for themselves.
7. Decorate the cover of the book to suit the verse.
8. Write a word or phrase on each page of the folded booklet. The booklet can be turned over so both sides of the paper can be written on.

other ideas:

- Make a cover from a rectangle of thin card stock folded in half. Make a template for a page shape that has its left side straight against the fold and its right side shaped, but with some of its folded edge remaining intact. Use a small amount of glue on the top and bottom pages of the accordion booklet, and place the booklet inside the folded card, as close to the fold as possible. Carefully remove any excess glue. Close the cover and press firmly. Then you will have a neat little booklet with shaped pages. Use a length of ribbon to tie the booklet closed if you wish.
- Design the accordion pleated booklet to fit into a small box, such as match boxes or gift boxes. Write on one side of the paper and stick the back page into the box. Fold the book carefully into the box and replace the lid. Decorate the box to suit the text.
- Use the accordion pleated designs or shelf edging paper to create a garland.

Ten Ways to Learn Memory Verses In Church

51. Dramatized Scripture Reading
52. PowerPoint Verse
53. Fabric Banners
54. Bulletin Verse Puzzle
55. Sermon Word Lotto
56. Verse Work Sheet Files
57. Responsive Readings, Greetings, and Blessings
58. Bulletin Covers/Posters
59. Verse Bags
60. Children's Stories

51. Dramatized Scripture Reading

Use with a variety of verses.

Supplies:

- a copy of *The Dramatized Bible* or your favorite Bible translation
- pencil and paper
- possibly a copier
- children willing to speak in church

Instructions:

1. Use a passage that is not too long and that can be used as a scripture reading at church in the near future. Look at the scripture reading and experiment with ways in which the verse could be creatively broken down and shared between different speakers.
2. Write a script for the passage, indicating the speaker for each part. The scripts created in *The Dramatized Bible* are ready for you to use.
3. Make several copies of the script, enough for each of the speakers to have their own copy.
4. Choose children who are willing to speak in church and can learn the verses by heart.
5. Give the children plenty of time to learn their parts. Practice the script together several times. Discuss the meaning of the verse together so the children are reading and learning with understanding.
6. Let them present the scripture reading together in church on the appropriate day.

Other ideas:

- Use a group of children, reciting simultaneously, to create a voice choir. This will mean that more children will be encouraged to learn the verses, and shy children can be involved more easily.
- Have the children dress up as characters in the scripture reading, or have them hold objects or pictures they have drawn that illustrate the passage they are presenting.

52. powerpoint verse

Use with a variety of verses, especially those that can be illustrated with attractive photographs.

supplies:

- computer and data projector (many churches use data projectors and computers in their worship service to project hymns, PowerPoints of the sermon, Bible verses, and announcements)
- appropriate software and cables, etc.

instructions:

1. Look for one verse in the scripture reading for the day that sums up the topic well and is a good verse for the children to learn.
2. Create an attractive PowerPoint slide that contains the verse in a clear, bold script that children can easily read. Include a bright picture that illustrates the verse in some way.
3. Ask the pastor if you can leave the memory verse on the screen so the children can look at the verse and memorize it during the sermon time.
4. Offer a small reward for every child who can recite the memory verse to the pastor as they leave the church.

other ideas:

- Make simple stickers using printable adhesive labels with the memory verse for the day. Add a small motif that illustrates the text. Many simple graphics programs enable you to print off sheets of stickers.
- Give each child a collector's card, and let them collect the verse stickers each week, as they try to learn them. Reward children for trying, not necessarily for a word perfect response, so they will continue to be encouraged and so you can involve children of all abilities.

53. Fabric Banners

Use with a variety of verses.

Supplies:

- a large piece of plain fabric hemmed on three sides with a channel stitched into the top edge
- a dowel or curtain rod to be inserted into the channel for hanging
- paper patterns for all the letters to be used on the banner—choose a simple computer font with chunky letters, size the letters to fit the banner you are creating, and print the patterns
- fusible web from a sewing store, plus iron and ironing board
- fabrics to suit the design of the banner
- pencils
- fabric scissors
- instructions for making banners available at www.worshipbanners.com (this will also link you to other useful banner sites)

Instructions:

1. Design a simple banner using the words of a short Bible verse and some simple illustrative graphics that suit the words or the theme.
2. Print the letter shapes, and draw simple patterns for the other fabric shapes that will make up the design.
3. Iron the fusible web with its backing paper onto the wrong side of the fabrics.
4. Draw the letters and shapes in reverse image on the fusible web backing paper, checking that the letters are all the same way up.
5. Give each child a fabric letter or shape to cut out if the children are old enough. They can use the outline you have drawn as their cutting line. They may need help to cut out the centers of the letters.
6. Let the children peel the backing paper off the letters and help you lay them on the banner in their final positions. Iron gentle creases into the fabric to give you straight lines for the lettering, if you wish.

7. Iron the letters and shapes onto the banner using the instructions on the fusible webbing package.

8. Hang the banner, and read the words together. The banner can be hung at home, in the children's Sabbath School room at church, or in the sanctuary. As the children see the banner, they will become familiar with the text.

Other ideas:

- Have the children help you to decide on the design for the banner after you have talked about the meaning of the verse.
- Have groups of children create different banners to cover a sequence of verses or verses on a related theme. You can create banners of Jesus' "I am" verses— the Bread of Life, Water of Life, Good Shepherd, Light of the World, etc. If they are all made the same size, these can create a beautiful series of banners to adorn a church sanctuary.
- Add embellishments and simple embroidery to the designs.
- Choose a verse about hands, and have each child draw around their hand on the fusible webbing paper. Then write their name on the palm of their fabric hand. These can then be ironed onto a banner.
- Give older children low count cross-stitch fabric so they can create mini banners, stitching the Bible verse and a simple design onto the fabric.
- Visit www.church-textiles.co.uk for more advanced inspiration.

54. Bulletin Verse Puzzle

Use with a variety of verses.

Supplies:

- a Bible verse that you want the children to learn
- access to the person who designs the bulletin
- pencils for the children

Instructions:

1. Ask the person who designs the bulletin to include a Bible verse in the bulletin that you want the children to learn.
2. List a few activities the children can do with any bulletin to help them learn the verse. Here are a few examples to help you get started:
3. Circle all the words in the bulletin that are also in the memory verse.
4. List all the first letters of every word in the memory verse. Find one letter in the bulletin that is the same as the first letter of the first word. Then draw a line from this letter to another letter in the bulletin that is the same as the first letter of the second word in the verse, and so on. Have a look at the shape that has been created by your line and see if it reminds you of anything.
5. Write out the memory verse on a separate paper. Cross out all the As in the verse, then all the Bs and so on until every letter in the verse has been crossed out. By then the verse should be very familiar!
6. Play "I spy" and find an object that begins with that letter for each initial of each word in the verse.

Other ideas:

- Work with the bulletin secretary to try and include all the words in the memory verse somewhere in the bulletin. This may take some creativity!
- Try putting an encoded verse in the bulletin for the older children to decipher.

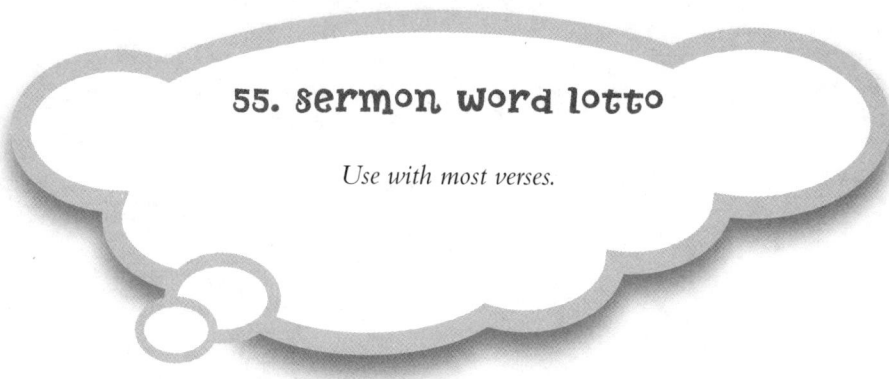

55. sermon word lotto

Use with most verses.

supplies:

- computer and printer
- Bible verse
- paper
- pencils

instructions:

1. Use a computer program to create a grid that has enough squares in it for every word in the memory verse and the Bible text. It is helpful if the verse relates to the sermon in some way.
2. Type one word of the memory verse into each of the grid boxes. Type them in the correct order so the children become familiar with the Bible verse as they do the activity.
3. Give each child a pencil and a copy of the Sermon Word Lotto sheet.
4. Ask the children to listen to the sermon. When they hear a word that is on their grid, they are to place a check mark in the box that contains that word. They keep adding check marks to the word boxes as often as they hear that word. The aim is to have one check mark in each of the word boxes by the end of the sermon, but this may not always be possible.
5. Try to discourage the children from standing up and shouting out when they have found all the words on their card!

other ideas:

- Create an empty grid using your computer. Print it on thin card stock and laminate it. This can then be recycled—the children can write different verses on their card each week with a wipe-off pen.

56. verse work sheet files

Use with a variety of verses.

supplies:

- one ring binder/loose-leaf file per child
- pencil, pen, and paper
- ruler and eraser
- photocopier and paper
- access to the Internet and copyright free Bible puzzle books to help create the work sheet

Instructions:

1. Label each binder with a child's name. Keep them at church to be collected on the way into the service and to be left behind afterward.
2. Add a different Bible verse work sheet each week for the children to do. Base the puzzles around a significant verse being used in the sermon. You will need to coordinate this with the pastor or speaker for the day.
3. Use all the resources you can find to help you create an interesting Bible verse work sheet. There are computer programs and Web sites that can help you create simple crossword and word search puzzles.
4. Include space and ideas for things children can draw in connection with the verse.
5. Use an outline font to create letters that can be colored in.
6. Add some questions that will help the children to think about what the text means to them and the difference it can make in their lives.
7. Copy one work sheet per binder for the children.

other ideas:

- Assign the design of the verse work sheet to a group of teens or young adults who like to make puzzles or who have good computer skills.

57. Responsive readings, greetings, and blessings

Use with verses that are also used as greetings and responses in your church's worship service.

Supplies:

- examples of responsive readings, songs, greetings, and blessings that are based on Bible verses

Instructions:

1. Use responsive readings, scripture songs, greetings, and blessings based on Bible verses as a regular part of your worship. As you incorporate these items into the worship service, the children will learn the Bible verses.
2. Help the children to realize that the words they are saying are also Bible verses, as these verses are usually used without their references.
3. Discuss the meanings of these responses in Sabbath School.

Other ideas:

- Involve the children in choosing or creating different Bible verse blessings and greetings for your church or writing a responsive reading.

58. Bulletin covers/posters

Use with a variety of verses.

Supplies:

- plain white paper
- crayons, markers, paints, etc.
- copies of the Bible verse (ideally, this verse should be a key verse for the service in which you are designing the bulletin cover)

Instructions:

1. Give each child a copy of the Bible verse that will be used in the service in a few weeks time.
2. Talk about what the verse might mean and how it could be illustrated.
3. Fold the white paper to the shape used for the bulletin. If space needs to be left for the date, name of the church, etc., then show the children how to leave a space or to shade that area very lightly.
4. Let the children create different designs that illustrate the Bible verse, making sure to include the words of the Bible verse.
5. Scan the finished pictures into a computer, and use them to create colorful bulletin covers.

Other ideas:

- Create a series of bulletin covers for special days, such as Christmas, Easter, Communion, Mothers' Day, Harvest, etc.
- Give each child a different verse to illustrate. Try to ensure that every child has a chance to design a bulletin cover if they wish.

59. Memory Verse Bags

Use with verses for which a range of activities are available or for which activities could be created.

Supplies:

- small cloth bags with handles sewn from scraps of fabric
- attractive printed laminated cards with different memory verses written on them
- puzzle cards based on the laminated memory verses and wipe off pens
- a collection of quiet child safe items related to the memory verse
- small books with stories related to the memory verse

Instructions:

1. Choose a selection of memory verses for the children to learn.
2. Make a few small cloth bags, coordinating the fabric to the verses, if at all possible.
3. Fill the bags with different items: puzzles, wipe off pens, books, and toys that are all connected with one memory verse. Make sure that a laminated memory verse card is included.
4. Let children choose a bag to explore when they come into church. Encourage them to learn the verse. When they have memorized the verse, they can choose a different verse bag the following week.

Other ideas:

- Work together as a group to make the bags, brainstorming ideas about what needs to go in each bag. Divide up the bags or the tasks to make the job easier.
- Ask different families to sponsor a bag, or have the teens make them for the younger children.
- Share the bags with children who are sick and/or in the hospital, as long as there is no danger of cross infection.
- Find puzzles and word searches connected with the Bible stories and verses by visiting www.mssscrafts.com.

60. children's stories

*Use with a variety of verses, depending on
the stories to be used.*

supplies:

- a positive, grace oriented children's story, object lesson, or simple experiment
- a Bible verse that sums up the theme of the children's story
- a creative way to teach the verse or to help the children experience the verse

instructions:

1. Reflect on the simple Bible verse that you have chosen. Think about how the children could experience the verse. Think about movement, taste, smell, sight, touch, and sound. Think about how the verse can come alive for the children in an interesting way.

2. Choose a way to teach the verse that suits the ages and abilities of the children in your church. You may choose to tell the children's story geared toward younger children but involve older children in learning the accompanying verse. Remember that most churches have a limited time for the children's story. Try to manage your activity within that time.

other ideas:

- Teach a Bible verse in an interesting way instead of telling a story, using illustrations or an experiment.
- Give the children a gift as they leave church, and stick a copy of the Bible verse on the gift so their parents can rehearse the verse with them on the way home. For example, a pot of soap bubbles can help a child to understand a verse about God's forgiveness and how He makes our sins disappear.

Ten Ways to Learn Memory Verses Using Objects

61. Still Life Verse
62. Verse Blocks
63. Purchased Bible Verse Items
64. Bandage Verse
65. Spirit Fruits
66. Egg Verse
67. Love Hearts
68. Place Mats
69. Dinner Table Frame
70. Walk Through a Verse

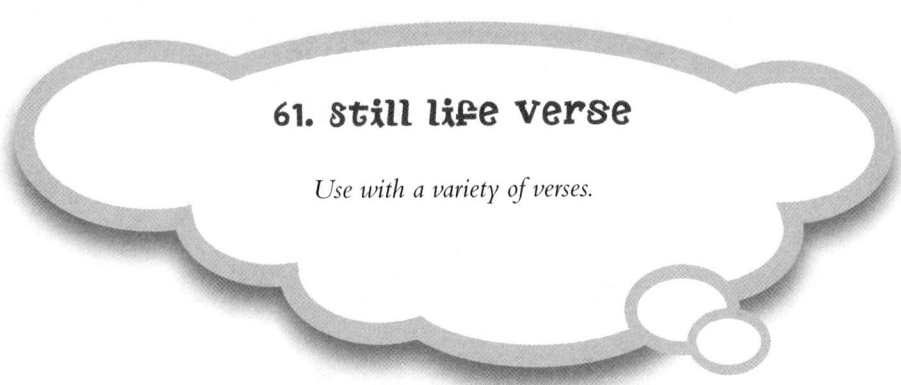

61. still life verse

Use with a variety of verses.

supplies:

- a card on which the Bible verse has been attractively written
- an assortment of objects to illustrate the verse
- some plain colored fabrics for the background
- camera (optional)

instructions:

1. Work together in groups of about four or as a family.
2. Talk together in the group about what the verse means.
3. Arrange a collection of objects (as artistically as possible) that illustrate the verse in some way. Think about what you hope people might learn from looking at the arrangement. What color background or cloth would you use in your arrangement? Where can you put the card when it's done?
4. View each other's arrangements.
5. Photograph the arrangements if you wish.

other ideas:

- Do this activity while on a picnic or at a camp, inviting groups of people to create their displays from anything they can find.
- Give each group different verses to illustrate centered around a specific theme, or divide a longer passage of scripture into sections.
- Use photographs of the arrangements to create a calendar that could be sold, a PowerPoint presentation for a worship service, or church bulletin covers, etc.
- Give the children the Bible verse card a week before this activity. Explain what they will be asked to do, and invite them to bring any items they think would help them to create a display to illustrate the verse.
- Create miniature verse arrangements using tiny things that can be turned into a permanent display in a basket, shadow box, or miniature showcase.

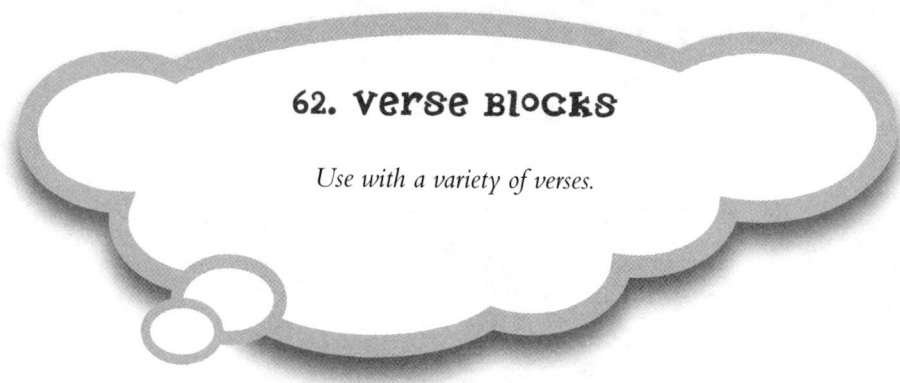

62. verse Blocks

Use with a variety of verses.

supplies:

- 16 plain lightly sanded wooden blocks from a craft shop
- acrylic paint in six different colors
- paintbrushes
- water for cleaning the brushes
- permanent markers
- six different Bible verses
- acrylic sealer

Instructions:

1. Paint each side of the wooden block a different color. When the paint is dry, turn the blocks so the upper sides of the blocks are all one color.
2. Write a Bible verse across the top of the blocks so every block is written on.
3. Turn the blocks so a different color is on the top surface, and repeat the process with a different verse until you have done this for all six sides.
4. Seal the surface of the blocks with an acrylic sealer by following the instructions on the can.
5. Let your child arrange and play with the blocks to read different Bible verses.

other ideas:

- Paint appropriate pictures on the blocks along with the words.
- Decoupage cutout pictures on the blocks.

63. Purchased Bible verse items

Use with any verses for which you can purchase suitable items.

Supplies:

- items from a Christian bookstore

Instructions:

1. Choose some tasteful and attractive items from the store that have Bible verses on them.
2. Place them in your home or Sabbath School classroom where they will be seen often.
3. Encourage your child to notice and read the words when you use the item or pass by it.

Other ideas:

- Try making some decorations, posters, or keepsakes using Bible verses.
- Find an artisan who can make an item for a special occasion and can incorporate a verse into the design that has special meaning to your children.
- Search on the Internet for Christian craftspeople, and commission them to create a special design for you

64. Bandage Verse

*Use with verses about healing
or binding up wounds.*

Supplies:

- torn strips of firm white cotton fabric
- ballpoint pens
- copies of the verse to be learned
- safety pins

Instructions:

1. Give each child a strip of fabric and the verse to be learned.
2. Let them write the verse on the strip of fabric using a ballpoint pen.
3. Let them bind something with the bandage, such as their wrist, reading the words of the verse as they wrap the bandage around their wrist. Or they could bind each other's wrists, to practice showing care for one another. Remind them not to wrap the bandage too tightly. Help them use the safety pins to fasten the ends.
4. Let them wear the bandage to remind them of the verse. If they forget the words, they can undo their bandage and check them again.

Other ideas:

- Make a few marks on the cloth with a red pen, paint, or marker to simulate blood from a wound.
- Cut out hearts from red poster board, and let the children bind a heart. Write the words of the verse on the heart so they are visible after the heart has been bound.

65. Spirit Fruits

Use with Galatians 5:22, 23,
learning about the fruits of the Spirit.

Supplies:

- a large bowl or basket
- as many different fruits as you can find to place in the bowl
- index cards with a different fruit of the Spirit written on each card

Instructions:

1. Talk about the different character qualities listed in these verses. What does it mean to love, to be joyful, peaceful, or patient?
2. Add the ideas about each fruit of the Spirit to the index card on which that quality has been written.
3. Look at the fruits in the bowl. Which fruit best represents love? Perhaps a strawberry might because it is red and heart shaped. Maybe a lemon could represent self-control. A pomegranate might represent patience because it can take patience to pick out the flesh.
4. Discuss the ideas together, and then make a display of the fruit, labeling each one for its chosen characteristic, and placing them in a line in the order in which they are listed in the verse.
5. Move along the line together, sharing or tasting one fruit at a time.

Other ideas:

- Let the children help to make a fruit salad or smoothie after labeling the fruits in verse order. While you are cooking, talk about how the Holy Spirit works in us to produce all these different fruits in our lives and how the combination can make all the fruits taste even better.

66. Egg Verse

*Use with verses about caring, gentleness,
or God's protection, etc.*

Supplies:

- one hard-boiled egg per child
- markers
- copies of the verse to be learned

Instructions:

1. Give each child an egg and a marker, and let them write the verse on an egg.
2. *Ask them to carry the egg with them for a day and to look after it carefully.*
3. Review the verse at the end of the allotted time, and let them talk about how this experience helped them to understand more about the verse they were learning.

Other ideas:

- Ask older children to look after their eggs for a week and to write a brief journal about their experiences with the eggs.

67. Love Hearts

Use with 1 Corinthians 13:4-8.

Supplies:

- an assortment of heart shaped objects, as many as you can find
- a copy of each of the phrases in 1 Corinthians 13:4-8 written on a separate index card

Instructions:

1. Shuffle the cards and place them face down in a pack.
2. Pick one card and talk about what the phrase means in the way we relate to each other on a daily basis.
3. Look at the hearts together and discuss which heart particularly illustrates the phrase. Talk about your different ideas. For example, "love is patient" could be illustrated by a lace or embroidered heart that would have required patience to make; "love is kind" could be illustrated by a heart made out of soft fabric, etc. It may be quite challenging to find hearts to match some love statements, but maybe you could talk about what kind of heart could illustrate the point, and perhaps you could make or find one that fits your ideas.
4. Make a display of the hearts and the cards, arranging the cards in the correct order for the verse and placing the different hearts with their cards.

Other ideas:

- Create a shadow box picture. Find very small hearts of similar sizes that illustrate the love texts. Write the love phrases on small labels or tags. Arrange the hearts and their labels in the box and glue them firmly in place. Hang the picture in your home, or give it as a wedding gift.

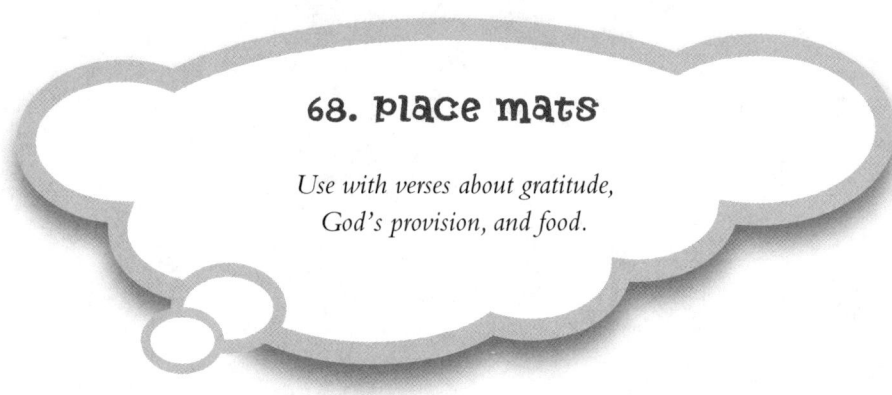

68. place mats

*Use with verses about gratitude,
God's provision, and food.*

supplies:

- different colored sheets of thin card stock that are place mat sized and will fit into laminating pouches
- markers
- stickers, paper shapes, and other thin and flat embellishments
- glue sticks
- laminating pouches and laminator
- copies of the verse to be learned

instructions:

1. Give each child a copy of the verse and a choice of colored card stock to make their place mat.
2. Let each child write the verse on their place mat and decorate the mat in any way they wish.
3. Laminate the place mats and let each child take their place mat home to use during the week. As they sit at the table to eat they will be reminded of their memory verse.

other ideas:

- Use fabric pens and fabric to create place mats instead of laminated cards. Follow the instructions on the fabric pens for your choice of fabric, preparing the fabric and sealing the paint with a hot iron.

69. Dinner table frame

Use with a variety of verses.

Supplies:

- a picture frame that can hold several pictures but reveals only one at a time
- attractive postcards with printed Bible verses or homemade cards with verses on them

Instructions:

1. Purchase a picture frame like the one described above. Some stand like a small easel and photos can be flipped from front to back to change the display. Others have a slide mechanism that automatically changes the pictures.
2. Fill every pocket or position in the frame with different verse cards.
3. Stand the frame on the dining room table or in another place where it will be seen often.
4. Flip to a new verse when everyone has learned it.

Other ideas:

- Create verse "graffiti." Use a clipboard and print off a Bible verse using a computer. If possible, use a background that looks like a brick wall and type the verse in white lettering, as if white paint has been used to paint the verse on the wall. Clip the verse to a clipboard and attach a white ink pen, which can be purchased from a craft shop. Place the verse where it will be seen, and invite family members to add their thoughts and ideas about the text in white ink on the "brick wall." This can be a useful way of involving a very active family in a shared devotional time, even if people are eating and leaving the home at different times.
- Purchase an acrylic photo cube and insert a verse into each side.

70. Walk through a verse

*Use a verse with several visual ideas
or a longer Bible passage, such as Psalm 23.*

Supplies:

- all kinds of objects, depending on the walk-through experience you want to create

Instructions:

1. Spend some time reflecting on the verse and how you could create a walk-through experience. Think about the different media elements that could be used to create a multisensory experience of the verse. It helps to brainstorm with someone else.
2. Gather the props you need and set it up. Try the activity for yourself and make adjustments.
3. Make sure that the words of the passage are clearly visible to those walking through, or play the words in a continuous audio or audio visual loop as the children slowly walk through the experience.
4. Talk about what the children learned after they finish the experience, and spend time reciting the verse together.

For example: If you are using Psalm 23, start with an image of a shepherd or a crook. Next, create a display of still water: mirror laid on the floor or table; green fabric around the edge shaped to look like grass for green pastures. The next area could be a place with lots of comfortable pillows, a place to rest and be restored. The valley of the shadow of death could be made from two tall panels with a narrow pathway between, big enough for two people to walk side by side. Drape black fabric over the panels and floor. When the child goes through the valley of death, have an adult go with them with a torch or something comforting. Later, the children come to a banquet table and choose something to eat, such as grapes or flat breads. Give each child a crown, or something else, to symbolize heaven.

Other ideas:

- Invite the church congregation to participate as part of a special program.

Ten Ways to Learn Memory Verses Using Actions and The Body

71. Stepping Stones
72. Run Around Verse
73. Word Relay
74. Verse Charade
75. Signed Verse
76. Handy Words
77. Beanbag Verse
78. Action Creation
79. Jump Up Verse
80. Alphabet Shapes

71. Stepping Stones

Use with verses about following Jesus or verses that suggest different shaped stepping stones.

Supplies:

- heavy paper
- thick markers
- scissors
- carpet tape or masking tape

Instructions:

1. Cut the paper into stepping stone shapes or other shapes suggested by the verse, such as footprints, birds, or hearts. Make them as big as the paper will allow.
2. Write one word of the verse on each paper shape. Make the word big and clear so it can be easily read.
3. Lay the paper shapes on the floor in a trail around the room, ensuring that they are in the correct order. Place them one step apart, so children can step from one shape to the next.
4. Tape the shapes firmly to the floor so they do not cause the children to slip. Check the tape before you use it to make sure it can be removed from the floor without leaving a residue or marking the surface.
5. Have the children step from one shape to the next, reading the words as they go.
6. Let them follow the trail several times until they have learned the verse.

Other ideas:

- Make the stepping stones out of craft foam, felt, or another material that does not slip on your floor surface.
- Cover the word on one of the stepping stones as the children go around the trail a second time so they have to remember the word for themselves. Continue covering more words until they are all hidden.
- Do this activity outside, and use sidewalk chalk to write the words on the ground.

72. Run around verse

*Use with verses about running,
moving, or searching.*

Supplies:

- paper
- markers or a computer and printer
- putty adhesive

Instructions:

1. Write or print each word of the memory verse on a different piece of paper. For long verses or passages, write several words on each sheet of paper.
2. Shuffle the pieces of paper so they are in a random sequence, and then stick them on the walls around the room.
3. Have the children learn the verse as a group. Once they have learned the verse, let them run around the room from one word to the next in the order in which the words appear in the verse.

Other ideas:

- Do this activity outside by pinning the words on trees.
- Place the words in different rooms of your house to encourage exploration and movement.

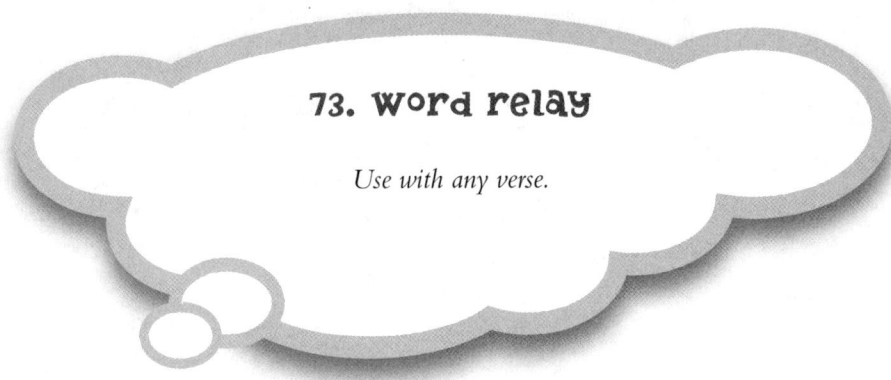

73. word relay

Use with any verse.

supplies:

- several sheets of thin card stock
- markers or a computer and printer
- putty adhesive
- large sheet of cardboard per group or a clear surface onto which the words can be stuck
- clean buckets or boxes

instructions:

1. Print the Bible verse onto the card stock and cut out each word separately, placing putty adhesive on the back of each card. You will need one set of cards per child or per team. If you have only one child, race him against the clock.
2. Place one set of words in each bucket or box, and line these up at the front of the room.
3. Divide the group into teams and give each team a surface or piece of cardboard on which to stick their words.
4. Spend a few moments teaching them the verse so they are familiar with the words and the order in which they need to be placed.
5. Form each team into a line and, when you blow a whistle, have one child from each team run to the bucket or box, take out a word, and run back to their team. As soon as the next person in line is touched by the runner, they can run and collect a word, and so on. Each person may need to run and collect a word more than once, so they need to be ready to run when it is their turn.
6. As the children are running and collecting words, the team also needs to be assembling the Bible verse in the correct order on their cardboard or plain surface.

Other ideas:

- Do this activity as a group if you do not want the children to compete against each other. It is good if there are enough words for every child to have a chance to run.
- Have several teams compete together against the clock. In other words, every team has to try and finish their verse within 10 minutes, or whatever is appropriate for the verse and your group.
- Insert the words, without the adhesive, into balloons so the balloons need to be popped to get the words out.
- Fish for the words by adding paper clips to the words and using a magnetic fishing rod.

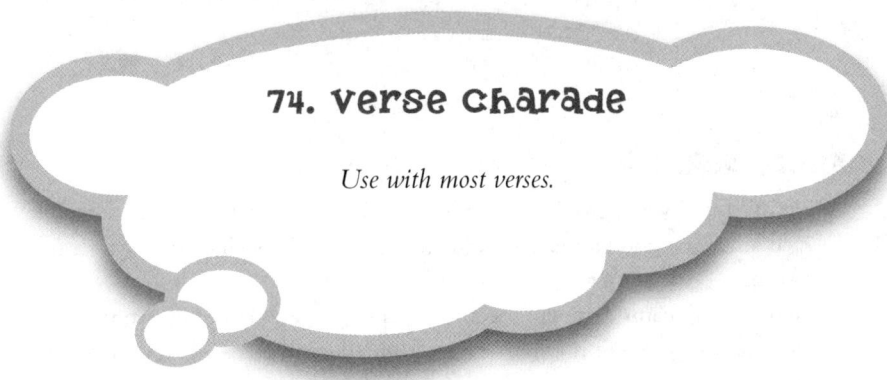

74. verse charade

Use with most verses.

supplies:

- active older children
- copies of different Bible verses

instructions:

1. Divide the children into two groups.
2. Give each group a different Bible verse. Make sure each group does not see the verse that the other group has been given.
3. Teach the children some basic moves for charades:
   - Number of words in the verse: Hold up the number of fingers.
   - Which word in the verse you are working on: Hold up the number of fingers again.
   - Number of syllables in the word: Lay the number of fingers on your arm.
   - Which syllable you're working on: Lay the number of fingers on your arm again.
   - Length of word: Make a "little" or "big" sign as if you were measuring a fish.
   - Sounds like: Cup your hand behind your ear.
   - Past tense: Wave your hand over your shoulder toward your back.
   - A letter of the alphabet: Move your hand in a tapping motion toward your arm (near the top of your forearm if the letter is near the beginning of the alphabet and near the tips of your fingers if the letter is near the end of the alphabet).
4. Allow each group a few minutes to decide how they will act out their verse using actions and mime so the other group can guess the verse. No one in the group presenting the charade is allowed to make any noise.
5. Let the children in each group take turns acting out some of the phrases or words in the verse for the other group to guess.

6. Allow each group a specific amount of time to present their verse.

Other ideas:

- See which group presents the verse that is guessed in the least amount of time. The winners are the best presenters rather than the best guessers.
- Have each team draw the words in their verse rather than act them out.

75. Signed Verse

Use with most verses.

Supplies:

- someone who knows sign language (it may be helpful if this person is also a hearing person)

Instructions:

1. Ask the signer to teach the children how to sign the Bible verse they are learning and to explain some of the signs used since they often have interesting origins.
2. Have the children practice the signs and the verse until they have learned them well.

Other ideas:

- Have the children sign the verse in church as a special presentation or in place of the scripture reading.
- Take a small group of children to visit a deaf person who signs, and have the children sign the verse for them. You could take pictures, cards, notes, and flowers to give to the person, too.

76. Handy Words

Use with verses about hands and actions.

Supplies:

- strips of paper about 1 cm. (½ in.) wide
- a copy of the words in the Bible verse divided into 10 segments and arranged so each section can be easily cut out
- scissors
- fine tipped markers
- tape

Instructions:

1. Give each child a copy of the words that have been arranged into 10 segments, and ask them to cut each segment apart.
2. Tape a loop of paper 1 cm. wide around, and slip the loops around all of the fingers and thumbs of each child.
3. Tape one segment of the verse to each of the fingers and thumbs so the verse can be read from left to right across the two hands with both palms up.
4. Practice reading the verse together with all segments visible.
5. Fold down a finger on each hand so its words cannot be seen, and practice the verse again. Keep folding down different fingers and trying to say the verse until all the fingers are folded down and the verse has been learned.

Other ideas:

- Use small pictures instead of words for some of the segments.
- Tear one finger loop off, instead of folding down a finger, until there are none left on the hand.
- Write the words on the fingers with a nontoxic washable pen instead of using the paper loops.

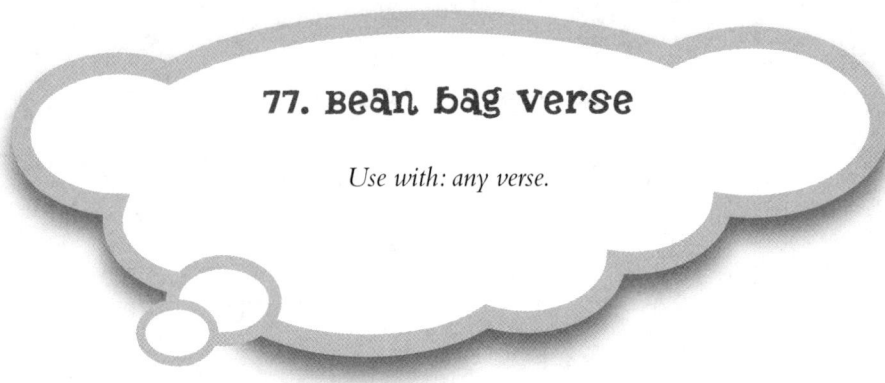

77. Bean Bag Verse

Use with: any verse.

Supplies:

- a bean bag

Instructions:

1. Sit the children in a circle and practice saying the memory verse together.
2. Explain the rules of the bean bag game once the children are familiar with the verse. You will begin the game by throwing a bean bag to someone. The child with the bean bag has to say the first word of the verse before throwing the bean bag to another child. Whoever the bean bag is thrown to has to say the next word in the verse. The bean bag can be thrown to anyone in the group.
3. Let the children practice, and then start the game.
4. See how quickly they can say the words as the bean bag is thrown from one person to the next.

Other ideas:

- Spin a bottle to select a person to say the next word.
- Have someone walk around the back of the group and touch people gently. As soon as someone is touched they have to say the next word in the verse.

78. Action Creation

Use with verses that contain action words.

Supplies:

- one Bible verse written clearly on a piece of paper per team

Instructions:

1. Divide the children into smaller teams if you have lots of children.
2. Give each team a verse, and ask them to create some actions for the words in the verse.
3. Give them time to learn the verse and to practice their actions.
4. Let each team demonstrate their verse to the rest of the group.

Other ideas:

- Give each group different verses from the same passage or on the same theme, or give each group the same verse to see how each team interprets the verse.

79. Jump Up Verses

Use with a variety of verses.

Supplies:

- a copy of the Bible verse for each child
- a red marker or yellow highlighter

Instructions:

1. Highlight a different word on each copy of the verse if you have a large group. If you have a small group or family, some children may have more than one word highlighted. Also, in a large group, several children may have the same word.
2. Practice saying the memory verse together with all the children sitting on chairs or on the floor.
3. Have them say the verse together slowly, and have each child jump up when his/her word is said.
4. Run through the verse again, but now, have the child who has the highlighted word jump up and say his/her word at the right point in the verse.

Other ideas:

- Have the children use a different response instead of jumping, such as raising their hand or holding up a placard with their word written on it.

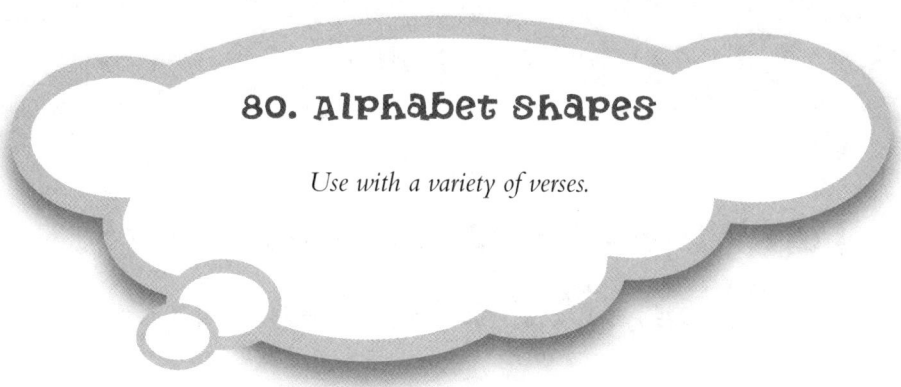

80. Alphabet Shapes

Use with a variety of verses.

Supplies:

- paper
- markers
- putty adhesive
- active and energetic children

Instructions:

1. Choose a verse that is not too long. Write each word on a different sheet of paper so it can be easily read.
2. Attach the words to the walls of the room in the order in which they appear in the verse.
3. Have the children practice making different letters of the alphabet with their bodies—they can choose uppercase or lowercase letters, whichever works best.
4. Stand a child or a group of children by each word. Have each group figure out how to make the first letter of their word using their bodies to make the shape.
5. Move the children to the next word in the sequence, and repeat the exercise. Continue until they have completed the full verse sequence at least once.

Other ideas:

- Have each group decide on a letter shape and teach the other groups how to make their letter. Then, have the whole group repeat the verse, shaping their bodies into the initial letter of each word. This will have to be done at a slower speed than you would normally say the verse.
- Create your own letter shapes together as a family, and practice them with the words in the verse until everyone has learned all the words.

Ten Ways to Learn Memory Verses Using Music and Sounds

81. Recycled Tunes
82. Clap-A-Verse
83. Scripture Songs
84. Background Music
85. Whispering Verses
86. Musical Verses
87. Musical Word Islands
88. Sound Swaps
89. Sound Effects
90. Buzz Alert

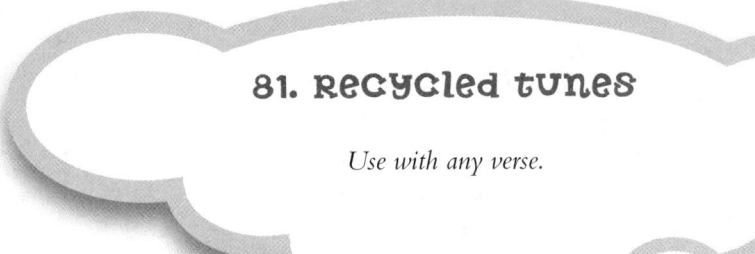

81. Recycled Tunes

Use with any verse.

Supplies:

- a supply of old tunes that most children in your culture will know, such as nursery songs, chorus tunes, or even theme tunes from popular, wholesome children's TV shows
- copies of the Bible verse to be learned

Instructions:

1. Sing the chosen verse to a few familiar and easy to sing tunes until you find one that fits well. It will be easier for them to learn the verse if they already know the tune.
2. Give the children copies of the text to be learned so they can read the words until they learn the song by heart.
3. Teach the children the song you have chosen.

Other ideas:

- Divide older children into groups, provide them with a copy of a Bible verse and see if they can find a popular tune that will fit the verse.
- Create two sets of cards. On one set of cards write some Bible verses to be learned, and on another set of cards write the names of some popular and easy tunes. Randomly assign each group one verse card and one tune card, and give them some time to practice their song. Let each group sing their verse as best they can to the tune they have been given.

82. clap-a-verse

Use with verses about clapping or hands or those verses with a natural rhythm.

supplies:

- lively hands
- a copy of the verse to be learned

Instructions:

1. Choose a verse that has a natural rhythm to the words. A good one to use is "Whatever your hand finds to do, do it with all your might" (Eccl. 9:10). You can clap this verse by clapping on the first beat of each line. As you clap, make each clap louder than the previous one till you are clapping with all your might.

- Whatever your
- Hand
- Finds to
- Do
- Do it
- With all your
- Might!

other ideas:

- Give the children a Bible verse, and ask them to create their own clapping pattern.

83. Scripture Songs

Use with a variety of verses, especially those for which scripture songs have already been composed.

Supplies:

- professional tapes, videos, DVDs, or CDs of scripture songs
- a suitable media player

Instructions:

1. Become familiar with the scripture songs available to you. When you need the children to learn a memory verse for which there is a good scripture song, let them listen to the song.
2. Practice singing the song with the children until they have learned the verse.

Other ideas:

- Play scripture songs when the children are arriving at Sabbath School, participating in a craft activity, or riding in the car. The children will soon learn the verses being sung.
- Play DVDs and videos of scripture songs between services at church.

84. Background Music

Use with a variety of verses.

Supplies:

- a range of different types of classical music on CD or tape, etc.
- several CD or cassette players
- several different Bible passages

Instructions:

1. Divide a large group into teams, or work together if you have a small group or family. This is a good activity for older children or young teens.
2. Choose a Bible passage and discuss it together. If you were to compose some background music for the passage, what would it sound like? What style of music would suit the passage best? Where would the mood of the music change?
3. Listen to some pieces of music and choose one that you think suits the verse the best. Match the moods of the music to a reading of the passage.

Other ideas:

- Read the chosen scripture in church, and use the chosen music as background music while the passage is being read.
- Create a PowerPoint presentation of the scripture passage that coordinates with the music and uses written words and images that express the meaning of the passage.

85. whispering verses

Use with any verse.

supplies:

- copies of several memory verses

instructions:

1. Sit the children in a line and whisper one of the memory verses to a child at the end of the row.
2. Ask the children to pass the whisper on by whispering the verse to each other as carefully as they can along the row.
3. Ask the child at the end of the row to recite the verse. See how much of it has been retained.

other ideas:

- Play this game in several teams if you have a large group. The team that can recite the verse with the least mistakes wins the game.
- Sit the children in a circle, and give several children in the circle a whisper to pass on. As they pass their whisper, they also pass a soft toy. They will know when their whisper has gone all the way around the circle when the soft toy arrives back in their hands. When the verse has passed around the circle, ask the children to compare the verse they started whispering with the one that was whispered to them.

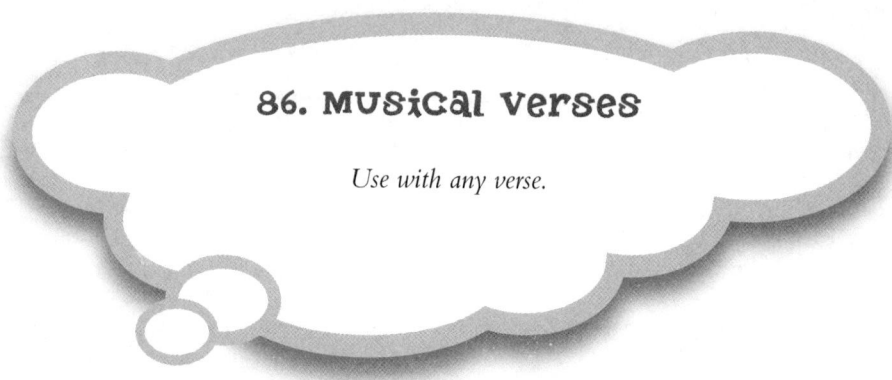

86. Musical Verses

Use with any verse.

Supplies:

- a Bible
- background music and CD player
- a circle of chairs

Instructions:

1. Sit the children in a circle and explain the game. The children are to carefully pass the Bible around the circle until the music stops. The child holding the Bible has to find the verse that is being learned and read it from the Bible. Explain the importance of handling the Bible reverently.
2. Play the game until every child has had a chance to find the verse and read it.

Please note: Be sensitive to the needs of children who find reading difficult. Make sure you have an adult to help the child whose turn it is so they experience success rather than failure and humiliation. The adult helper can offer extra tips and prompts to help the child.

Other ideas:

- Review a series of verses by playing this game in a different way. When the music stops, call out a Bible text, and see if the child can find the verse you have called out. Or, you could name the verse without the reference and see if the child can remember the reference and find the verse in the Bible.

87. Musical Word Islands

Use with any verse.

Supplies:

- large pieces of wallpaper
- scissors
- thick markers
- masking tape
- background music and CD player

Instructions:

1. Write each word of the verse on the wrong side of a piece of wallpaper. Make the piece big enough for the whole group to stand on if possible.
2. Tape each piece of wallpaper to the floor so it will not slip and children will not trip on the edges.
3. Help the children learn the verse so they know in which order the words will come.
4. Explain the rules of the game: The children will walk in a circle around the edge of the room as the music plays. Whenever the music stops, all the children have to walk as quickly as they can and stand on the piece of paper that contains the first word in the verse. The next time the music stops the children have to go to the second word, and so on until the verse is complete. No one is disqualified from the game for arriving at a word island last or for getting a word wrong.
5. Keep all the children in the game till the end because the goal of the game is to learn the words, not win the game.

Other ideas:

- Make word signs and stick them around the room. Have the children run to the sign instead of running to a piece of paper on the floor.
- Play the game outside by writing the words on the ground with sidewalk chalk.

88. Sound Swaps

Use with verses about praise and music.

Supplies:

- a variety of different sound making objects such as shakers, slide whistles, maracas, small bells, etc.
- copies of the Bible verse to be learned

Instructions:

1. Practice saying the verse with the children until they have learned it fairly well.
2. Swap out some of the words in the verse for sounds. For example, each time the word "love" is said the little bells are rung, or when the word "down" is said, the slide whistle is used to make a sound that seems to slide down. You can swap as many words for sounds as you like.
3. Give the sound makers to the children, and help them practice making their sound when their word is said.
4. Practice the verse together by adding the sounds and saying the words at the same time.
5. Practice until you can use the sound instead of the word. The children will have to listen carefully so they know when to make their sound.

Other ideas:

- Use noises that the children can make with their mouths and body, such as clapping, clicking, and stomping, instead of using instruments to make the sounds.

89. Sound Effects

Use with any verse with potential sound effects.

Supplies:

- a selection of items that make different sound effects
- copies of the Bible verse to be learned

Instructions:

1. Work together as a family, or divide children into groups with an adult.
2. Explore the chosen Bible verse together, and think about some sound effects for the verse. How many sound effects can the group come up with for a short verse?
3. Practice reading the verse in unison. Each person should take responsibility for one of the different sound effects while the verse is being read.
4. Perform the verses for each other.

Other ideas:

- Have older children work alone to create their own sound effects for a verse, and have them perform for each other.
- Generate sound effects using different computer programs, or download sounds from copyright free Web sites.

90. BUZZ Alert

Use with any verse.

Supplies:

- a buzzer, whistle, or loud bell

Instructions:

1. Teach the children the memory verse until they have learned it well.
2. Give them a task that can easily be interrupted, such as a craft activity.
3. Tell them that whenever they hear the buzzer they need to stop what they are doing, stand up, put their hands in the air, and recite the memory verse they have learned.
4. Do this a few times to keep the group alert and to practice the verse.

Other ideas:

- Use a quiet signal or code word instead of a loud noise. Whenever the children hear the signal or word, they have to respond by reciting the text.
- Use the signal at times when the children are not expecting it to see if they can still recall the verse.

Ten Ways to Learn Memory Verses Around The Home

91. Edible Verses

92. Stairway Verses

93. Mirror Verses

94. Voice Memo

95. Phone Texting/Messaging

96. Computer Graphic Design

97. Picture Cups

98. Verse Bunting

99. Door Labels

100. Stenciled Verses

91. Edible Verses

Use with any verse, especially those about food.

Supplies:

- a variety of the following items:
- small alphabet cutters and cheese or soy cheese slices
- edible writing gel or tubes of frosting with narrow nozzles
- alphabet candies, cookies, pretzels
- cupcakes, graham crackers, or crackers
- pizza or large frosted cake

Instructions:

1. Choose a verse that doesn't have too many words.
2. Choose food that will be suitable for everyone in your group. Check beforehand for food intolerances, special diets, and allergies.
3. Choose a way to write the verse that fits the food and the edible writing materials available to you, such as tomato pizza or crackers with cheese letters, frosted cupcakes with candy letters, peanut butter crackers with gel letters, etc.
4. Invite the children to help create the verse by cutting the letters, selecting the candies, or piping the writing gel onto individual crackers or cupcakes. This activity helps the children become familiar with the words.
5. Assemble the food so everyone can see the whole verse, and learn the verse together.
6. Take turns saying the verse without looking at the edible words. Each time someone can say the verse, let him/her choose a food item to eat.
7. Continue until each person has had a chance to say the verse and eat a "word."

Other ideas:

- Create the first letter of each word as a prompt to the full word if the verse is too long or if you have limited materials.

- Conduct this activity at a picnic or party.
- Look for supplies at a sugar craft store. A specialist store will carry alphabet cutters and printable edible paper that allows you to print off the words, cut them out, and apply them to food.
- Let the children write the words of the verse on paper flags used to identify different kinds of sandwiches, or fold adhesive labels around toothpicks to make little flags on which words can be written. Flags can then be inserted into muffins, bagels, fruit pieces, or whatever is appropriate.

92. Stairway Verses

Use with any verse, especially those about growing closer to God.

Supplies:

- paper
- a computer and printer or markers
- scissors
- masking tape

Instructions:

1. Print each word of the verse on a separate sheet of paper that is in landscape orientation (the longest sides are at the top and bottom of the page). Have your child help you do this.
2. Cut the words so they fit comfortably onto the riser of your stairs (the upright sections between the steps.
3. Divide the words between the risers so the words are in order from the bottom of the stairs to the top.
4. Encourage your child to read the verse each time he/she walks up the stairs.
5. Have your child practice pausing on each step and saying the word below him/her without looking at it.

Other ideas:

- Write the words on the risers of concrete steps outside with sidewalk chalk.

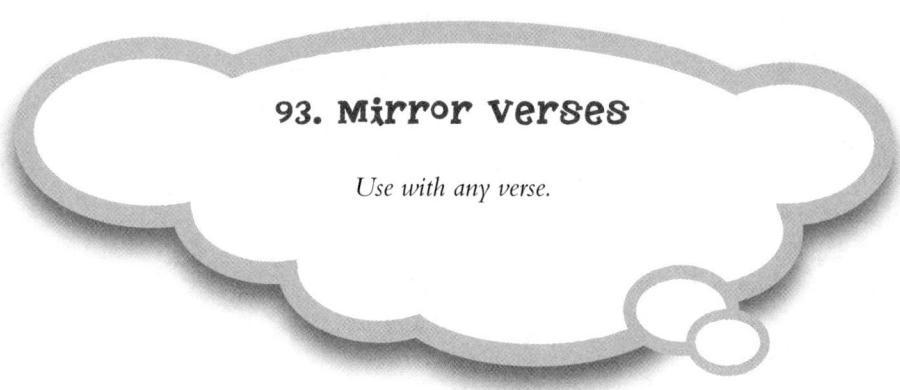

93. Mirror Verses

Use with any verse.

Supplies:

- wipe off markers or lipstick
- old cloth or paper towel for wiping the words off the mirror

Instructions:

1. Write a verse on a mirror that everyone uses. Use a wipe off marker or lipstick.
2. Take turns wiping off one word each day. By the time the verse has disappeared, everyone should have learned the verse.

Other ideas:

- Use a chalkboard and chalk instead of a mirror.
- Use children's soap crayons and write on the tiles in a bathroom. One word could be wiped off each time someone has a bath.

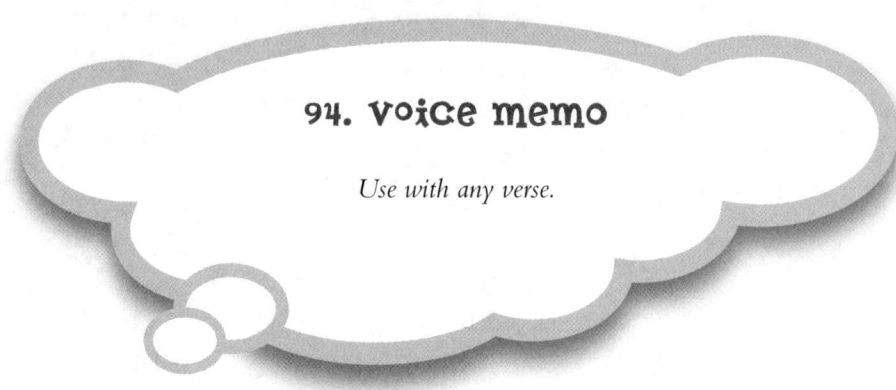

94. voice memo

Use with any verse.

supplies:

- something that can record a few seconds of speech, such as a voice memo, Dictaphone, message recorder, voice recording picture frame, key ring, or toy

instructions:

1. Show your children how to record their voice on the voice recorder. Help them record the memory verse.
2. Let them activate the message whenever they like or according to a schedule, depending on where the message can play back. For example, if the verse has been recorded in a teddy bear, perhaps they would like to activate the message at bedtime.
3. Let them record another verse once the first one has been learned.

other ideas:

- Purchase a small portable voice device, such as novelty recording key rings, that enables your child to play the verse throughout the day.

95. Phone texting/messaging

Use with any verse.

Supplies:

- a cell phone with texting capability

Instructions:

1. Send your child a text message with the Bible verse to be learned. This can then be read discretely at any time during the day.

Other ideas:

- Encourage your child to text you the memory verse. The texting process will help to reinforce the words.
- Send your child an e-mail with the verse. Perhaps the verse could be e-mailed as a message on a Christian e-card that illustrates the verse, or maybe you could find an e-card design that already includes the text being learned.

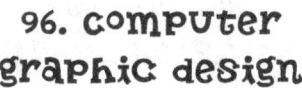

96. computer graphic design

Use with a variety of verses.

supplies:

- a computer with graphics program
- color printer
- paper, card, printable T-shirt design paper, etc.
- other craft items as required

instructions:

1. Choose a Bible verse to be learned.
2. Brainstorm about how the verse could be printed on a product, such as a poster, framed picture, laminated place mat, T-shirt, bag, bookmark, or writing paper.
3. Use a graphics program to create something that has the Bible verse appropriately incorporated into the design.
4. Produce your designs. (Don't forget to reverse your design if you are printing words onto printable T-shirt design paper, otherwise your words will come out in mirror image and be much harder to read.)

other ideas:

- Create items to sell, and use the proceeds to support your favorite charity.
- Check the copyright and user regulations to make sure you don't break any copyright laws.
- Search the Internet for ideas by exploring Christian e-card and T-shirt sites (www.dayspring.com, www.crosscards.com, www.religioustshirts.co.uk).

97. Picture Cups

Use with any verse, especially those about food and drink or God's provision and blessing.

Supplies:

- a clear plastic mug that comes apart so different paper designs can be created and inserted into its wall (these are often available at craft stores)
- paper
- markers

Instructions:

1. Help your child write the memory verse on the plain side of a sheet of paper cut to fit inside the cup.
2. Let your child decorate the paper to illustrate the text.
3. Slide the paper into the cup, and assemble the cup so the paper is protected inside the cup wall and visible through the transparent plastic section.
4. Let your child use the cup at meal times. Wash the cup by hand to protect the design.

Other ideas:

- Change the verse as often as desired.
- Use special porcelain markers to write a verse on a ceramic mug, which can then be baked to make the design permanent. A family could create a series of verse mugs to help them learn different Bible verses.

98. verse bunting

Use with most verses, especially those about praise and celebration.

supplies:

- brightly colored paper
- markers
- scissors
- glue sticks
- ribbon or string

Instructions:

1. Cut the brightly colored paper into identical pennant shaped triangles. The children can help cut the triangle shapes if you make a template from stiff card.
2. Fold over a small amount on the short side of each triangle and stick them along a length of ribbon or string to create a bunting (strings of flags used for celebrations). Alternate the colors.
3. Write one word of the memory verse on each flag of the bunting. Hang the bunting where everyone can see it.

other ideas:

- Create a smaller version to be used as shelf edging or hung in a smaller space.
- Print the words using a computer and printer; then cut the triangles.

99. Door labels

Use with verses that link with different activities in the home.

Supplies:

- precut wooden door plaques (available from a craft store)
- pots of acrylic paint
- fine tipped permanent markers in different colors
- paper and pencils
- embellishments such as buttons and other flat backed decorative items that suit the texts being created

Instructions:

1. Choose texts that connect with the room for which you are making a door label, such as texts about rest for a quiet room, eating and food for dining rooms and kitchens, washing for bathrooms, and sleep for bedrooms, etc.
2. Draft a simple design on a piece of paper the same size as the door plaque to check the size and spacing of words, pictures, and embellishments.
3. Prepare the wood according to the paint directions, and then paint the plaque a background color.
4. Write the verse carefully onto the plaque using the fine tipped permanent markers.
5. Decorate the plaque with painted designs or stick on embellishments.
6. Seal the surface of the plaque with a protective coating.
7. Attach it to the door.

Other ideas:

- Do this as a family project. Even small children can help to paint the base coat on a plaque and stick on the embellishments.

- Print off verses using a printer, and decoupage them to the plaque if you don't have confidence in your lettering skills. Some craft stores sell Bible verse rub-down transfers or stickers that you could use.
- Have a door labeling celebration, and plan a short activity that illustrates the relevant text before unveiling the door plaque for that room.
- Let the children choose their favorite verse, and help them create a plaque for the door of their room.

100. stenciled verse

*Use with verses about God's grace and love
and good ways of living together.*

supplies:

- a lettering stencil, preferably one designed for painting on walls
- stencil brush
- stencil paint
- palette
- pencil
- ruler and spirit level
- low tack masking tape

instructions:

1. Choose a text that is cheerful and encouraging and that you want permanently stenciled on a wall in one of your rooms, maybe a child's bedroom.
2. Practice stenciling on some scrap paper. The best way to stencil without making a mess is to swirl the brush through a tiny drop of paint on a palette, and then dab the excess paint off on the palette until it seems like there is almost no paint left on the bristles. Then swirl the brush firmly over the letter stencil until the letter is as dark as you want. Less paint is better than more, and you will soon be able to judge how much paint you need on the brush.
3. Draw a faint line on the wall with a pencil to help keep your lettering straight, though you can choose to make your lettering curve in attractive designs as well. Plot out where each word will start and finish, using your stencil to help you. Adjust your design if necessary.
4. Stencil your chosen text onto the wall, and add other stenciled images to your design.

other ideas:

- Create a border for your room. Print your chosen verse using a computer and printer and a font that gives you the outlines of simple letters. Use a good quality paper and print using a horizontal banner option, if you have one. This feature enables you to print a longer verse over several sheets of paper that you can then trim or overlap. You can also add images to your design, or even print it in color. Let your children color in the words on the border and add other pictures if they wish. Then paste the border on the wall as you would apply a wallpaper border.

- Create a printed border for your room, and use putty adhesive to attach it to the wall. This option will allow you to change or remove the border when you wish to do so.
- Create an outline printed verse border, and attach it to the wall at a height your children can reach. Let your children color the border whenever they wish. Make sure your children understand that this is the only place where they can color on the wall!